MISSION SUSTAINABLE INDIA

MISSION SUSTAINABLE INDIA

GRIHA SHIKSHA KENDRA

Published by Zorba Books, August 2022

Website: www.zorbabooks.com
Email: info@zorbabooks.com

Title:- Mission Sustainable India, Volume-3

Printbook ISBN:- 978-93-93029-76-8
Ebook ISBN:- 978-93-93029-82-9

Zorba Books Pvt. Ltd. (opc)
Sushant Arcade,
Next to Courtyard Marriot,
Sushant Lok 1, Gurgaon – 122009, India

A Vision Document on

Mission Sustainable India

(Volume-3 of 4)

A Vision Document-

Conceived, Coordinated and Compiled By:

Sunil Sood

Email: sunilsolar@yahoo.co.in Mobile: 7739802112

In collaboration with:

- Arvind Rastogi
- Neelamegan R
- Udhayakumar B.V.
- R. Vaidyanathan
- Ms. Indu Sinha
- Sandeep Nisal
- Pramod Srinivas

An inititaive by

Supporting Organizations

ECONAUR

The Volume-3 of Vision Document on "Mission Sustainable India" has been published with the financial contributions from the following organisations and individuals:

A. List of Organisations:

1. Polybond Insulation Private Limited
2. Activa Engineering, Nagpur
3. Swain and Sons Power Tech Private Limited

B. List of Individuals:

Sl. No.	Name	Location	Mobile No.
1.	Dr. P P Mittal	Delhi	9811402040
2.	Sandieep Nisal	Nagpur	93708 67249
3.	Yusuf Bhetasiwala	Mumbai	9820019338
4.	N. Ravishankar	Chennai	9444557741
5.	Udhayakumar B.V.	Dindigul	9650139995
6.	Saif Kureshi	Ahmedabad	9426622829
7.	Maheshwar Prasad	Patna	9470063368
8.	Ulhas Vajre	Thane	9821672242
9.	Mr. Tiger Aster	Hyderabad	9588663075
10.	Prakash Ashtunkar	Nagpur	9823137713
11.	Sanjay G. Bhagat	Nagpur	9028734320
12.	Dr. Shaikh Shamser Ali	Chennai	9380389123
13.	Krishna Das Bairagi	Ujjain	9907270259

CONTENTS

ACKNOWLEDGEMENTS

I'd like to express my deepest thanks to Shri Arvind Rastogi, Shri Neelamegan R., Shri Udhayakumar B.V., Shri R. Vaidyanathan, Ms. Indu Sinha and Shri Sandeep Nisal for the research and writing support provided.

My special regards to Shri Saumya P. Garnaik, Petron, IAEMP for writing the Foreword.

I am thankful to Indian Association of Energy Managements Professionals for supporting the Mission and taking up the responsibility as a leading organisation.

Thanks to all donors and advertisers for supporting the publication with financial contributions.

Last but not the least, I would like to extend my deepest gratitude to the volunteers of Mission Sustainable India for their continuous support.

(Sunil Kumar Sood)

National Convener, Mission Sustainable India

FOREWORD

We are standing at the cross-roads of the challenge of sustaining our rapid economic growth while dealing with the global threat of climate change. India's development path is based on the country's unique resource endowments, the overriding priority of economic and social development and poverty eradication, and India's adherence to the legacy of its civilization that places a high value on the environment and maintenance of ecological balance. This climate change may alter the distribution and quality of India's natural resources and adversely affect the livelihood of its people.

With an economy closely tied to its natural resource base and climate-sensitive sectors such as agriculture, water, and forestry, India may face a major threat because of the projected changes in climate essentially on account of the historical, cumulative, and excessively large impact of the large carbon footprint of the developed countries. While engaged with the international community to collectively and cooperatively deal with this threat, India needs a national strategy first to adapt to climate change and secondly to enhance the ecological sustainability of India's development path.

For example, the rejuvenation of mixed landscapes and promoting water conservation through natural farming practices & afforestation are again strong initiatives that could preserve nature to carry forward into the next generation. The biggest trademark for ensuring the sustainability of these practices is their affordability & availability. For instance, developing *last-mile connectivity* through Electric Two-Wheelers is a great initiative ensuring better accessibility and sustainable mobility.

Interventions in the form of proper integration of sustainable sources of electricity, generated through solar, hydropower, and wind sources would ensure the availability of electricity in the most remote locations of the country establishing energy security. The target for sustainability in India should focus on energy security in the long run. The Government of India has laid its emphasis on ensuring *Atmanirbharata* or self-reliance in India, a core factor of which lies in promoting energy security in the next years to come.

I am happy that Indian Association of Energy Management Professionals (IAEMP) has adopted the Vision Document on "Mission Sustainable India" and is leading the movement with an objective of involving all sections of society, economic sectors, environmentalists, institutions, citizens in India's tryst with sustainability. The basic tenet of the mission is to ensure sustainable growth through an appropriate mix of Energy, Efficiency, Equity, and Environment. I request everyone to support the Mission.

(Soumya P. Garnaik)

Patron Member, IAEMP

PREFACE

The Volume-1 of the Vision Document on Mission Sustainable India covered topics of Sustainable Citizenship, Governance, Bureaucracy, and Justice System.

In the Volume -2, we covered additional topics such as Mass Media Communication, Sustainable Education, Sustainable Habitat, Sustainable Food and Health Systems.

The Volume-3 of the Vision Document takes forward the Mission to important technical topics of energy, water, transportation, manufacturing and tourism.

The Chapter-12 on Sustainable Energy focusses on the importance of demand side management with energy conservation and efficiency measures as it also suggests a policy which covers short term, medium term and long term sustainability of supply side options. The Chapter also talks of effective engagement of energy management professionals certified by the Bureau of Energy Efficiency under the Energy Conservation Act, 2001.

The Chapter-13 on Sustainable Water mentions the importance of Energy-Water-Food Nexus. It elaborates the Water Pyramid approach for sustainable availability of water for all purposes.

The topic of Sustainable Transportation has been exhaustively covered in Chapter-14 and gives some innovative ideas.

The Chpater-15 covers the topic of Sustainable Manufacturing and Production. Most of the points are quite well known already however, there was need to put them in a systematic manner for better implementation which has been done in this Chapter.

The last chapter under the Volume-3 on Sustainable Tourism gives some innovative ideas which have the potential to become the most effective to take India towards a Sustainable Development path.

We look forward to active support from every one.

Team Mission Sustainable India

12

SUSTAINABLE ENERGY

Highlights:

- Finalize short term, medium terms and long term "Energy Policies"
- Give top priority to Energy Conservation & Efficiency
- Implement greatly-improved technologies for harnessing the fossil and nuclear fuels, to ensure that their use, if continued, creates much lower environmental and social impact.
- Develop and deploy the truly renewable energy sources on a much wider scale.
- Innovate for major improvements in the efficiency of energy conversion, distribution and end use of energy

Sustainable energy is the practice of using energy in a way that "meets the needs of the present without compromising the ability of future generations to meet their own needs."

When referring to methods of producing energy, the term "sustainable energy" is often used interchangeably with the term "renewable energy". In general, renewable energy sources such as solar, wind, and hydroelectric energy are widely considered to be sustainable. However, particular renewable energy projects, such as the clearing of forests for the production of biofuels, can lead to similar or even worse environmental damage when compared to using fossil fuel energy. Nuclear power is a zero emission source and while its sustainability is debated, the European Union has chosen it to be the part of a low-carbon energy backbone by 2050.

Moderate amounts of wind and solar energy, which are intermittent energy sources, can be integrated into the electrical grid without additional infrastructure such as grid energy storage. These sources generated 7.5% of worldwide electricity in 2018, a share that has grown rapidly. As of 2020, costs of wind, solar, and batteries are projected to continue falling.

12.0 Why Sustainable Energy Matters

One of the greatest challenges facing humanity during the twenty-first century must surely be that of giving everyone on the planet access to safe, clean and sustainable energy supplies.

Throughout history, the use of energy has been central to the functioning and development of human societies. But during the nineteenth and twentieth centuries, humanity learned how to harness the highly-concentrated forms of energy contained within fossil fuels. These provided the power that drove the industrial revolution, bringing unparalleled increases in affluence and productivity to millions of people throughout the world. As we enter the third millennium, however, there is a growing realisation that the world's energy systems will need to be changed radically if they are to supply our energy needs sustainably on a long-term basis.

The world's current energy systems have been built around the many advantages of fossil fuels, and we now depend overwhelmingly upon them. Concerns that supplies will 'run out' in the short-to-medium term have probably been exaggerated, thanks to the continued discovery of new reserves and the application of increasingly-advanced exploration technologies. Nevertheless it remains the case that fossil fuel reserves are ultimately finite. In the long term they will eventually become depleted and substitutes will have to be found.

Moreover, fossil fuels have been concentrated by natural processes in relatively few countries. Two-thirds of the world's proven oil reserves, for example, are located in the Middle East and North Africa. This concentration of scarce resources has already led to major world crises and conflicts, such as the 1970s 'oil crisis' and the Gulf War in the 1990s. It has the potential to create similar, or even more severe, problems in the future.

Substantial rises in the price of oil also can cause world-wide economic disruption and lead to widespread protests, as seen in the USA and Europe in 2000.

The exploitation of fossil fuel resources entails significant health hazards. These can occur in the course of their extraction from the earth, for example in coal mining accidents or fires on oil or gas drilling rigs.

They can also occur during distribution, for example in oil spillages from tankers that pollute beaches and kill wildlife; or on combustion, which generates atmospheric pollutants such as sulphur dioxide and oxides of nitrogen that are detrimental to the environment and to health.

Fossil fuel combustion also generates very large quantities of carbon dioxide (CO_2), the most important anthropogenic (human-induced) greenhouse gas. The majority of the world's scientists now believe that anthropogenic greenhouse gas emissions are causing the earth's temperature to increase at a rate unprecedented since the ending of the last ice age. This is very likely to cause significant changes in the world's climate system, leading to disruption of agriculture and ecosystems, to sea level rises that could overwhelm some low-lying countries, and to accelerated melting of glaciers and polar ice.

Rising global temperatures have already caused significant melting of ice around the North Pole, which is now accessible to ships at certain times of the year. This does not affect global sea levels, since most Arctic ice is floating. But if ice at the South pole, much of which is based on land, were to melt, this would cause very substantial rises in sea levels

Nuclear power has grown in importance since its inception just after World War II and now supplies some 7 per cent of world primary energy. A major advantage of nuclear power plants, in contrast with fossil fuelled plants, is that they do not emit greenhouse gases. Also, supplies of uranium, the principal nuclear fuel, are sufficient for many decades – and possibly centuries – of supply at current use rates.

However the use of nuclear energy, as we shall see, gives rise to problems arising from the routine emissions of radioactive substances, difficulties of radioactive waste disposal, and dangers from the proliferation of nuclear weapons material. To these must be added the possibility of major nuclear accidents which, though highly unlikely, could be catastrophic in their effects. Although some of these problems may be amenable to solution in the longer-term, such solutions have not yet been fully developed.

Extracting energy from fossil or nuclear fuels, in the course of providing energy-related services to society, generates significant environmental and social impacts. These impacts are greater than they need be because of the low efficiency of our current systems for delivering energy, converting it into forms appropriate for specific tasks, and utilizing it in our homes, machinery, appliances and vehicles. An important way of mitigating the environmental impacts of current fuel use is therefore to improve the efficiency of these systems. Over the past few decades, significant efficiency improvements have indeed been made, but further major improvements are feasible technologically – and are, in many cases, attractive economically.

Of course, not all energy sources are of fossil or nuclear origin. The renewable energy sources, principally solar energy and its derivatives in the form of bioenergy, hydroelectricity, wind and wave power, are increasingly considered likely to play an important role in the sustainable energy systems of the future. The 'renewables' are based on energy flows that are replenished by natural processes, and so do not become depleted with use as do fossil or nuclear fuels – although there may be other constraints on their use. The environmental impacts of renewable energy sources vary, but they are generally much lower than those of conventional fuels. However, the current costs of renewable energy sources are in many cases higher than those of conventional sources, and this has until recently retarded their deployment.

12.1 India Energy Scenario

With a population of 1.4 billion and one of the world's fastest-growing major economies, India will be vital for the future of the global energy markets. The Government of India has made impressive progress in recent years in increasing citizens' access to electricity and clean cooking. It has also successfully implemented a range of energy market reforms and carried out a huge amount of renewable electricity deployment, notably in solar energy. Looking ahead, the government has laid out an ambitious vision to bring secure, affordable and sustainable energy to all its citizens.

India has made huge strides to ensure full access to electricity, bringing power to more than 700 million people since 2000. It is pursuing a very ambitious deployment of renewable energy, notably solar, and has boosted energy efficiency through innovative programmes such as replacing incandescent light bulbs with LEDs (under the Ujala scheme). And it is addressing the serious health problems caused by air pollution for its major cities, providing 80 million households with liquefied petroleum gas connection (under the PradhanMantriUjjwalaYojana scheme), thereby reducing the exposure from biomass cooking stoves, a major cause of respiratory diseases.

India is also introducing important energy pricing reforms in the coal, oil, gas, and electricity sectors which are fundamental to further opening the energy market and improving its financial health. It is taking significant steps to enhance its energy security by fostering domestic production through the most significant upstream reform of India's Hydrocarbon Exploration and Licensing Policy (HELP) and building up dedicated oil emergency stocks in the form of a strategic petroleum reserve. The scale of these achievements is hard to overstate.

12.2 The Indian Energy Sector - A Sustainable way Forward

Energy is a key driver for agriculture, industries, and service sectors that influence economic development, but today's rising concern over its sustainability has put India in a critical position. The burning of fossil fuels causes multiple environmental problems such as air pollution and global climate change. Global change threatens the very existence of life.

Transforming the present coal dominated energy mix to renewable and sustainable energy dominated energy use is one of the herculean tasks facing India. A fine balance of environmental sustainability with necessary economic development is required. On the other hand, the transition to sustainable and renewable energy technologies provides an opportunity to address not only the environmental problems but also overall economic and developmental needs to improve the living standards of people with equity and economic sustainability.

All these considerations suggest that in creating a sustainable energy future for India during the coming decades, it will be necessary:

1. to implement greatly-improved technologies for harnessing the fossil and nuclear fuels, to ensure that their use, if continued, creates much lower environmental and social impact;

2. to develop and deploy the renewable energy sources on a much wider scale; and
3. to make major improvements in the efficiency of energy conversion, distribution and end use.

The above 3 points are under the active consideration of the Government of India. India's new energy policy is under finalization. Recently, International Energy Agency (IEA) has published "India 2020 Energy Policy Review and suggested that the Government of India should:

- Establish permanent energy policy co-ordination in the central government, with an overarching national energy policy framework to support the development of a secure, sustainable and affordable energy system.
- Continue to encourage investment in Indias energy sector by: > ensuring full non-discriminatory access to energy transport networks > working with the states to implement power sector and tariff policy reforms with a focus on smooth integration of variable renewable energy and power system flexibility > moving from government allocation of energy supplies to allocation by market pricing > further rationalising subsidies and cross-subsidies.
- Prioritise actions to foster greater energy security by: > reinforcing oil emergency response measures with larger dedicated emergency stocks and improved procedures, including demand-restraint action and proper analysis of risks by using oil disruption scenarios and capitalising on international engagement > strengthening the resilience of Indias energy infrastructure, based on a robust analysis of the water energy nexus and cooling demand, notably when planning future investment.

- Improve the collection, consistency, transparency and availability of energy data across the energy system at central and state government levels.
- Adopt a co-ordinated cross-government strategy for energy RD&D, which enables impact-oriented measurement and dissemination of results.
- Ensure Indias international energy collaboration continues to be strong and mutually beneficial, highlighting the countrys energy successes and supporting continued opportunities to learn from international best practices.

It is expected that the new Energy Policy will be finalized soon incorporating all good suggestions from the sustainability point of view.

12.3 Mission Sustainable India Approach for Sustainable Energy Supply

We suggest the "Energy Pyramid "approach for achieving sustainable energy targets. The energy pyramid helps us in fixing priorities and action plans by starting at the end users of energy. It interlinks the roles of energy conservation, efficiency and renewable energy to minimize the dependence on fossil fuels. It also helps in our understanding of conservation and efficiency.

'Conservation' and 'Efficiency' are separate concepts although closely related. Energy Efficiency is making something that does the same function, but uses less energy, for example a BEE 5 star rated refrigerator consumes less energy than a 1 star refrigerator. Energy conservation requires being modest and smart in use of appliances, gadgets and equipment consuming energy to the desired levels as per the need.

It is possible to use an inefficient appliance/equipment intelligently and smartly to reduce energy consumption; while at the same time an efficient appliance can be used carelessly to actually increase the overall energy consumption. Conservation techniques require productive use of resources and the ability to do something well or achieve a desired result without wasted energy or efforts.

Energy conservation and Energy efficiency are presently the most powerful tools to realize our dream of Sustainable Energy. As depicted in Fig-1, if we have to switch over entirely to renewable energy in future, (A mix of Hydel, Wind, Biomass, and Solar etc.) then we must build it on 'Conservation' techniques and 'Efficiency' as the foundation blocks. 'Unlimited Renewable Energy' is just a wishful thinking. Whatever form of energy we use today, or tomorrow; it has to have the support and backing of "Conservation' and 'Efficiency'. This concept has been explained with the help of an 'Energy Pyramid' (Fig-1). The applications of the this concept in our residential buildings has been shown in Fig-2 (Page-31)

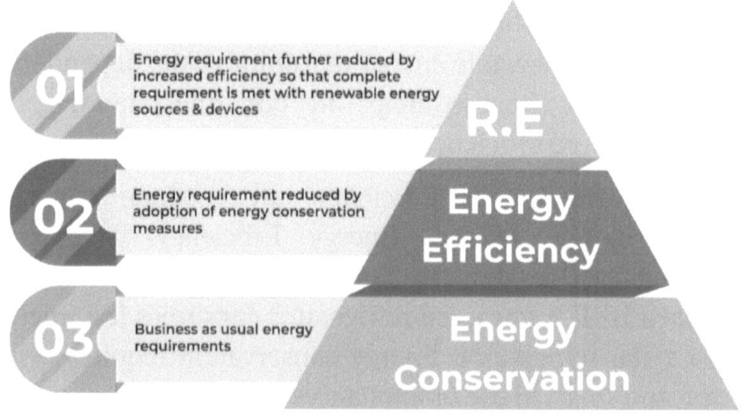

Energy Pyramid (Fig-1)

The idea of the pyramid is that to efficiently control and ideally reduce energy consumption you start with the least cost option (energy conservation) as the base and work toward the highest cost option (renewable energy). The energy pyramid is a basic but effective diagram outlining how renewable energy, energy efficiency, and energy conservation should work together to accomplish our clean and sustainable energy aims. Energy conservation is significant for sustainable future. Factors such as technical, institutional, financial, managerial, pricing policy and information diffusion affect energy conservation programs.

Energy conservation is one of the important elements of sustainable frameworks and models. Many sustainability projects focus especially on conservation. Energy conservation decreases the savings possible through energy efficiency developments. Increased energy conservation is a critical element of sustainable future. Energy conservation means decreasing energy use by voluntary human effort to save energy. Decreased energy consumption through conservation can utilize not only energy consumers by decreasing their energy costs, but also the society. High energy prices act to hold energy costs down by incentive energy conservation. Energy conservation increase energy efficiency and can frequently be the most cost-effective and reliable option, if applied correctly.

An important reduction in consumer energy costs can happen if energy conservation measures are adopted properly. The payback period for many energy conservation projects is many times less than a few months. Energy conservation includes the development of energy efficiency, the formulation of pricing policies, good industrial practices, and good load management strategies. Pricing policies play an important role in sustainable development. The development of energy conservation may lower the price of energy sources and make them more affordable

The need for energy is one of the biggest challenges ahead. The global energy demand will increase by 36% by 2035 with the increasing population. As energy consumption increases, dependence on energy is increasing. The pollution that occurs throughout the production process is at the forefront of privileged issues that need to be tackled around the world. For this reason, safe and environmentally sustainable, cost effective global energy solutions should be increased. In the context of sustainable development goals, countries are determined to use their energy resources in a way that will make them efficient, efficient and least effective for the environment.

Energy efficiency policies are one of the areas that need to be addressed sensitively because of the direct relationship between the sustainability of economic growth and social development objectives and the key role played by reducing total GHG emissions. Excessive use of energy causes the rapid depletion of natural resources, the pollution of the environment, and the payment of money at a high rate for energy. Energy conservation is energy efficient use without any reduction in production, comfort, and workforce.

Energy conservation is absolutely useful to the environment, as a unit of energy not consumed equates to a unit of resources saved and a unit of pollution not produced. Policy has an important role in supporting energy conservation in any society since not only can it produce an adequate economic environment that finally leads to savings, but it may also impose regulations for proper energy management, promote recycling and energy recovery, and encourage suitable education of the society.

12.3.1 Engagement of Certified Energy Auditors and Energy Managers

Although the concepts of energy conservation and efficiency did emerge way back during the first world war itself to conserve precious energy resources , in India, these concepts were first taken up seriously only after the oil price shocks during 1970s. A number of steps were taken by the Central Government to contain the rapidly rising bill on import of petroleum products.

Realizing that the voluntary efforts have not helped much to promote energy conservation and efficiency, the need for statutory measures was felt by the government and action to prepare a comprehensive legislation was initiated some times in the year 1995. It took about 4-5 years to prepare a draft legislation which was introduced as Energy Conservation Bill in the Parliament in the year 2000 and in the year 2001,it was passed as 'The Energy Conservation Act, 2001 to *provide for efficient use of energy and its conservation and for matters connected therewith or incidental thereto*.

Bureau of Efficiency (BEE) under the Ministry of Power, Government of India was established on 1st March, 2002 under the Energy Conservation Act, 2001 (As amended in 2010). The section 13 of the EC Act elaborates the 'Powers and Functions of BEE'. Besides, performing many of the tasks assigned to it under the Act, BEE has been conducting national level examination for certification of energy managers and energy auditors.

The first examination was conducted in the year 2004 and since then 20 examinations have been conducted so far and the 21st is scheduled in the month of September, 2021. It is estimated that more than 40,000 candidates have already appeared for the examination and about half of them have passed the examination and remaining are under various stages of clearing the certification process.

The initiative of the certification process by BEE has been appreciated by everyone as it has opened up new avenues for acquiring professional qualification for engineers, scientists and architects. We are of the opinion that there is a need for more than 100,000 certified energy auditors and managers to make India an 'Energy Efficient Nation' and contribute maximum possible towards reduction in emission of GHG gases due to reduced consumption of fossil fuels.

The various groups of BEE certified energy auditors (CEAs) and energy managers (CEMs) such as "Indian Association of Energy Management Professionals" and "BEE FRIENDS" have given some suggestions on how the cadre of CEA/CEMs. Some of the suggestions are described below:

Suggestion No 1- Engaging CEA/CEMs as "Energy Efficiency Coordinators"

We suggest that the CEA/CEMs Individual free-lance and employed in PSUs, Industries and Educational Institutions may be engaged by BEE for the activities elaborated in the following paragraphs. Such persons may be given a designation of "Energy Efficiency Coordinators" (EECs) by BEE and engaged for all voluntary schemes and programmes on some honorarium basis.

1. Dissemination of Information

BEE/SDAs are required to take all measures to create awareness and disseminate information for efficient use of energy and its conservation (clause e, section 13, clause e, and section 15). They can empanel CEA/CEMs as "Energy Efficiency Coordinators" at "Ward, District and State Levels" for Domestic, Commercial and Industrial sectors including MSMEs, ULBs, PSUs, Government offices and institutions etc. BEE and SDAs can jointly formulate a long term scheme for this purpose.

2. Collection of Primary Data/Baseline studies

BEE/SDAs need regular support for collection of primary data from domestic and commercial user of energy and resources which is not readily available from other sources. EECs can do the sample surveys and provide highly useful primary data. Such data will help in not only preparing the "Energy Plans" but will also be useful in identifying the improvements needed as well as for research purposes.

3. Organizing Training Programmes

All programmes aimed for training of personnel and specialists in the techniques for efficient use of energy and its conservation (clause f, section 13, clause f section15) can be organized by the EECs with the help of experts.

4. Strengthening of Consultancy Services and Life Long Learning programmes

BEE has to take initiative to strengthen consultancy services in the field of energy conservation (clause g, section 13). Energy Efficiency Coordinators with different subject and sector expertise can be involved as faculty members.

Suggestion-2: Engaging CEA/CEMs under the provisions of the EC Act,2001

To provide for a minimum sustainable business and dignity of profession, we suggest that BEE/SDAs may engage Individuals/Small energy management firms working on full time for certain provisions of the EC Act, 2001 as elaborated below:

1. Promoting Research & Development

BEE, as per clause (h), section 13 ; has to take initiative to promote research and development in the field of energy conservation. This is one area where CEA/CEMs can really do wonders in association with BEE/SDAs. R & D may be in equipment or process design or its application.

2. Setting-up of Demonstration Projects

This is another potential area which can be served by CEA/CEMs. They can be involved in implementation of pilot projects and demonstration projects for promotion of efficient use of energy and its conservation (clause j, section 13)

3. Promoting Innovative Financing

Any technology or equipment which at first glance looks financially unviable becomes viable with the help of suitable innovative financing mechanism. CEA/CEMs can help BEE in meeting its objective as per clause l, section 13 of the EC Act on promoting innovative financing mechanism

4. Providing feedback and follow-up services

BEE/SDAs will need regular feedback from the designated consumers on various issues such as labeling (clause d, section 14) action taken on recommendation of accredited energy auditor (section k, section 14) updating and follow-up for action taken for norms for processes and energy consumption standards for equipment and appliances (clause n, section 14)

5. Preferential treatment for energy efficient equipment/ appliances

BEE/SDAs will need to take step to encourage preferential treatment for use of energy efficient equipment/appliances (clause section 14 and clause g section 15). CEA/CEMs can ensure this by introducing life cycle cost purchase policy.

6. Matters to be included for the purpose of inspection

CEAs can help the SERCs for the purpose of inspection (clause i, section 15) and take up responsibilities to assist inspectors to be appointed under the section 17

7. Technical backup on Standards & labeling Programme

BEE has launched a massive nationwide S & L Programme. There is a need for third party verification of the claims of the manufacturer. CEAs/CEMs can be involved for such verifications and to suggest improvements in S & L Proramme.

Suggestion-3: Exploring engagement of CEA/CEMs for schemes and programmes of other Central and State Ministries

We suggest that BEE may advice Ministry of Power to proactively apply the provisions of clauses (t), (u) and (v) of section-14 of the EC Act, 2001 and issue necessary guidelines to different relevant ministries indirectly related to efficient use of energy and its conservation and recommend to them to involve CEA/CEMs in their national and international schemes and programmes. A list of such ministries is given below:

1. Ministry of Jal Shakti
2. Ministry of Environment, Forests and Climate Change
3. Ministry of New & Renewable Energy
4. Ministry of Heavy Industries and Public Enterprises
5. Ministry of Petroleum and Natural Gas
6. Ministry of Micro, Small and Medium Enterprises
7. Ministry of Agriculture and Farmers Welfare
8. Ministry of Commerce and Industry
9. Ministry of Food Processing Industries
10. Ministry of Science and Technology
11. Ministry of Skill Development and Entrepreneurship
12. Ministry of Education
13. Ministry of Housing and Urban Affairs

Suggestion-4: Introduction of Energy & Resources Demand Assessment Study Scheme

BEE has a promotional scheme for all stake holders except for the projects under planning. This suggestion is to address the need for a third party look for planning of energy and resources for new projects/under planning stage.

A close look in to our annual budget reveals that major share of the planned and un-planned expenditure is incurred on purchase of equipment/items/systems which consume energy and resources not only during their manufacture but also during operation and maintenance. The same holds good for all private projects too. The planning and execution of these projects goes through various stages such as preparation of feasibility reports, detailed project reports, basic and detailed engineering and finalization of specifications of various items and equipment. Though these functions are carried out by the panel of persons specialised in their respective fields or by respective consultants, none of these activities are normally scrutinised by a competent third party expert who is trained and tuned to look at the whole process from energy & resources efficiency point of view. The final purchase decision is still on the initial cost basis and not on the life cycle cost basis.

During the energy audit studies we have experienced that various utility equipment and systems like air conditioning and ventilation systems, air compressors, boilers and steam piping, DG sets etc. are often selected keeping very high safety margins of over 100 – 200 % in both capacities and quantities. This results in un-necessary expenditures on the oversized and extra items, as huge sums of money are blocked in procuring the same while in some cases more important items are left out.

With a pool of highly experienced CEA/CEMs available, a scheme on the concept of 'Energy & Resources Demand Assessment (ERDA) may be introduced by BEE. Under the ERDA concept, the complete planning process compulsorily is vetted by independent experts to review the final selection from the view point of energy and resources efficiency.

The ERDA study will basically include intense scrutiny of the items/equipment/systems planned as a pre- requisite of a project to be set up in respect of their capacity, quantity, and other specifications. This is carried out with a view to ensure its best performance, utility and adequacy. It involves value analysis in which the specification of the equipment are checked whether they suite the infra-structure requirements.

Hence, in this process the over sizing or even under sizing of the equipment is avoided. All in all, it helps in the selection of appropriate technological and utility equipment as far as their specification and quantities are concerned. The whole exercise results in bringing down the energy & resources requirement.

In other words ERDA studies will help the project implementation authorities to decide about the adequacy of and necessity of an engineering item or equipment before they are ordered.

Suggestion-5: BEE's initiative on Sustainable Development for Gated Communities and Apartment complexes

The trend of gated communities is growing now with more than 50% of the population in Metros living in Gated communities. Such communities have a system of being governed by a "Resident Welfare Association". The office bearers are often busy in attending to many issues and for them the security and safety is of prime importance. Such communities use energy and resources quite inefficiently and there is none to provide them guidance and technical support.

We suggest that BEE takes an initiative on all India basis involving the CEA/CEMs directly to introduce a voluntary scheme whereby the communities can appoint a CEA/CEM on part time basis as their "Community Energy & Resources Manager" (CERM). BEE may initially (for 2 years) provide a fixed financial assistance linked with the present energy and resources consumption bills. CERM can also coordinate with local agencies as well as to create awareness in the community on sustainable development concepts.

Once the communities realise that it is beneficial to have a CERM as their part time basis, they will certainly continue to appoint CERM even paying from their own funds. New project promoters of Gated communities can also be included in the scheme so that the sustainability.

12.4 Saving Electricity at Homes for Sustainability

Electricity is a secondary form of energy which can be generated by using primary sources of energy like Coal, Oil & Gas, Hydro, Nuclear or Renewable Energy like Solar, Biomass, Wind etc. We need energy to produce and cook food, light and cool/heat our homes, run appliances in our homes. Electricity is also needed for transport, industry, commercial, institutional, recreational, medical and governmental activities. Electricity is the costliest but the cleanest and highest quality energy and can be used to do all types of works which no other forms of energy can do. It is said that in future everything will be done with electricity only. Hence, we should try to learn and adopt the best practices to use electricity intelligently and smartly.

12.4.1 Why should we save electricity?

Electricity is directly linked with the **3 dimensions of sustainability**

- Economic
- Social
- Environmental.

This makes it very important that we use electricity efficiently and judiciously. Saving electricity not only helps us in reducing our bills but also results in several benefits to the society, nation and the planet. Some of the benefits are listed below:

Economic Benefits:

Electricity is produced in power plants which require huge capital investments by the government and the public. Then there are recurring expenses for fuel, maintenance, salaries etc. The losses in generation, transmission, distribution add to the cost. The country is spending more than 10 Lakh Crores per year on electricity. It costs 2 times more to generate than to save same amount of electricity. The electricity cannot be stored also (except in batteries; which again adds to costs) it is therefore economically more prudent to use electricity smartly and intelligently.

Social Benefits:

10-15% of our population; mostly in rural areas is still not having access to electricity and they are dependent on polluting fuel Kerosene to light their homes. By saving electricity, we can share the same with the underprivileged population. The availability of electricity will help in social benefits to the rural population. Their children can get better education and health facilities. By making electricity available to them, their economy also improves as they can work for longer hours.

Environmental Benefits:

The efficient use of electricity will help in lesser emission of CO2 and other Green house gases and particulate matters. With more emphasis on electrification of transport sector, the pollution in cities will reduce.

From the above, we can understand how important it is to save electricity. It is possible to do so by using electricity intelligently and smartly without sacrificing on comfort etc.

12.4.2 How can we save electricity?

Basically, electricity can be saved in 3 different ways:

- Conservation Measures- These measures require understanding of how each electricity consuming item needs to be used. There are Dos and Don'ts and certain techniques which must be explained to all family members and followed strictly.
- Efficiency Measures- These measures require retrofitting of existing inefficient gadgets/appliances with the highest efficiency ones available in the market. These measures are implemented with external help and still need to be monitored.
- Renewable Energy Measures- These measures require replacing electricity consuming gadgets with solar energy based gadgets and also need external help and expert advice.

12.4.3 ABC approach to save electricity

It is recommended to adopt ABC approach i.e. Accounting, Budgeting (Best Practices) and Controlling for maximum benefits.

Accounting of Electricity Consumption:

We should start with understanding how the billing is done and how much electricity is consumed by which item or appliance. Basic understanding of what is the meaning of a unit of electricity (kWh) and how it is calculated is very important. The billing is in two parts i.e Fixed Charges and Energy Charges. Fixed charges depend on the connected load and Energy charges are levied on actual consumption as per gradually increasing slab tariff. The step by step guide on how to account electricity consumption is given below:

1. Open a file to keep records of electricity bills
2. Safety First-understand all electricity safety measures before starting. Do not attempt anything which requires services of a qualified electrician.
3. Understand how the electricity meter works and start taking meter readings twice a day i.e at 7 am and at 7 pm to see the consumption pattern in day time and night time.
4. Make a list of all electricity consuming items in the home with their rated power in watts
5. Estimate the approximate hours of use.
6. Enter the data in an Excel sheet in the following format

Sl. No	**Item Descrip-tion**	**Rated Power (w)**	**Estimated Hours of Use (Hr) per day**	**Consum-ption per day wHr (3 X4)**	**Consum-ption per month (5) X No. of days**
1	2	3	4	5	6
1.					
2.					
3.					
4.					
5.					

It may be noted that the items like Refrigerators, ACs, and Geysers are provided with thermostats which switches off the compressor/heating element once the set temperature has been achieved. Further, Ceiling fans are provided with regulators and as such consumption depends on the regulator setting. Such appliances need more analysis to account their consumption. The following steps may be adopted to estimate approximate consumption of such appliances:

- Switch off everything – check the meter, it should not be working.
- Note down the initial meter reading
- set the thermostat/regulator Fridge/AC/Fans etc at middle point
- Start the appliance and keep it running for minimum of 2 hours
- Note down the meter reading again
- The difference is the approximate consumption by the appliance for 2 hours. Multiply it by the no of hours it is used to get the daily consumption.

One may repeat the exercise in the night hours and at different settings of thermostat for better results. Similar calculations shall also be carried in different seasons.

Coming back to point (vi) above, the estimated monthly electricity consumption thus arrived should be compared with the bill to ensure that the meter is working properly and to identify the potential electricity saving measures.

Best Practices for electricity savings:

As explained earlier, the electricity savings can be realized by the adoption of conservation, efficiency and renewable energy measures. Understanding the best practices in the adoption of such measures helps in maximizing gains. Some of the best practices are listed below:

Conservation Measures:

- Basic rules to ensures switching off lights/fans/ACs etc. when not in use should be kept in mind
- Teach the family members about the losses due to 'Standby consumers' (Ghost Consumers) and instruct them to switch off electronic gadgets from main Switch instead of Remote.
- Set computers on power saving mode.
- Clean Lighting Fixtures, Ceiling Fans, and Filters & Coils of ACs regularly.
- Make use of day lighting and 'free cooling' (opening the windows) as much as possible.
- Ensure that appliances are used smartly and intelligently e.g.- set thermostat of Fridge as per weather conditions/ load. Read the user's instruction manuals and follow the guidelines given. Sometimes the manufacturers will give insufficient/wrong information. Double check the instructions and adopt them to suit your usage.
- Avoid using appliances during peak load hours (morning and evenings). Use during late night (after 10 pm) or early morning (before 6 am) to reduce peak demand. This will also keep your electric wiring in healthy condition.
- Use ACs at a higher thermostat setting along with a Super energy efficient Ceiling Fan i.e. 27-28 Deg.C.

- Make use of Timer Sleep Mode settings for ACs and Fans (Super energy efficient fans with remote come with this facility)
- Adopt 'Task-Lighting & Cooling' wherever possible.
- Use hand operated tools as much as possible instead of Mixer/Grinder

Efficiency Measures:

- Discontinue the use of Incandescent Lamps and Compact Fluorescent Lamps (CFLs)- replace them with Light Emitting Diode (LED) Lamps.
- The so-called 'zero watt' bulbs actually consume 10-15 watts -replace it with 0.5 watt LED lamp.
- Provide 2-3 watt LED Lamps for areas where low illumination will suffice.
- Provide 5 watt LED lamps for small rooms, bath rooms, toilets etc
- Replace all T8 and T12 Fluorescent tube lights with LED tube lights.
- Replace old ceiling fans with 28/35 watt super energy efficient fans.
- Provide Sensors to automatically switch off lights/Fans etc when not in use.
- Replace Electric Geyser with Solar Water Heater
- Make it a policy to always buy highest efficiency latest gadgets. For example-whenever AC is to be purchased buy latest Inverter type AC or the ones coming with highest star rating.

Renewable Energy Measures:

- Replace Electric Geyser with Solar Water Heater
- Use Solar Lanterns and Torches regularly or install a Solar Home-lighting system.
- Use Solar DC fan for cooling requirements during power cuts instead of providing an Inverter.
- Make use of solar passive techniques to minimize the use of electrical appliances for cooling/heating etc.

Controlling:

Once a system is in place to introduce all measures to save electricity, it becomes important to ensure that this is followed religiously by all members of the family. This part can be made interesting and rewarding by introducing an Incentive and penalty scheme. A piggy bank may be kept for this purpose and any member found wasting electricity may be fined a sum equal to potential loss in a month and asked to deposit that much money in the piggy bank. The money thus collected may be used partly to fund purchase of new energy efficient gadget and partly to have an outing for the family.

12.5 Energy Conservation in Travel

1. Before buying a Car – think twice- Just calculate how much it would cost you per KM travel in next 5 years! Think of the hidden costs- insurance, road tax, parking fees, depreciation, maintenance and so on....you may then prefer to utilize the services of 'Chauffeur' driven Public Transport or even Auto/Taxi.
2. If you must buy a car, Buy a second hand car instead of a new one. Choose a more fuel-efficient vehicle

3. If you already have a Car, please follow the advice given by the Petroleum Conservation Research Association (PCRA):

    - Drive only at 40-50 km/hour (may not be possible in traffic congestion but may be possible in certain routes)
    - Fill up when the tank is half full to minimize evaporation losses.
    - Use the right gear
    - Keep your engine tuned
    - Don't wait for your car to warm up; instead, drive in low gear till the engine warms up. Use choke briefly only when necessary.
    - Stop-and-go driving wastes fuel. When you slam on the brakes, a lot of useful energy is wasted in the form of heat. A good driver always anticipates stops.
    - Keep your foot off the clutch
    - Clean air filter regularly
    - Use the recommended grade of oil
    - Choose low-traffic routes
    - Reduce load on the car
    - Minimize travel by planning the trip and combining tasks.
    - Check your tyres weekly for the correct air pressure.
    - Avoid idling your vehicle at signals and traffic jams: Ten seconds of idling uses more fuel than in restarting the vehicle.

4. Use bicycle or two-wheeler for local work like shopping.
5. Arrange car pools for going to work and for taking kids to school
6. Avoid air travel and go by train instead.
7. Buy locally grown and produced foods. Avoid food items that have been imported or have come from long distances. They would have consumed considerable energy on transport.
8. Live near your place of study or work, if possible.

12.6 Energy Conservation in Cooking

1. Eat as much as Raw vegetables as possible. Add more fruits in your diet.
2. Eat together to avoid repeated heating of food. Encourage pool diner/lunch in your friend circle.
3. If you have a solar water heater in your home-use the hot water in summer for cooking rice & dal or for warming of frozen food etc..
4. Keep the burners clean. Buy a spare burner so that the same is kept ready for change over when the one under use needs cleaning.
5. Soak rice and cereals before you start cooking. Keep vegetables and other items ready for cooking before lighting the burner.
6. Use Pressure cooker with multiple containers as much as possible- this way you can cook 2-3 dishes at a time.
7. Cover cooking vessel with lid. Use only the required amount of water.

8. Use the small burner as far as possible and reduce flame at the right stage.
9. If you have a terrace with good Sun shine-buy a solar cooker. Solar cooked food will not only save fuel but will also be good for health. If you use it intelligently, it can even save time for you!.

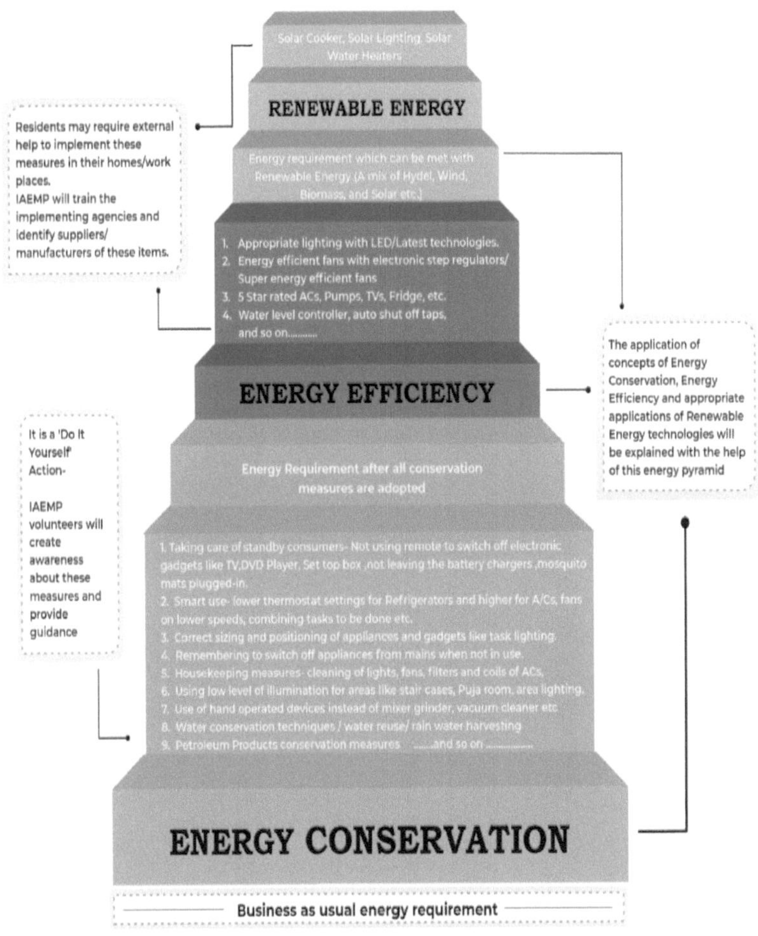

Sustainable Energy Pyramid for Residential Buildings

Fig-2

13

Sustainable Water

Highlights:

- Focus on Water-Energy-Food Nexus Approach
- Adoption of Water Pyramid Approach to promote conservation and efficient use of water
- Protection and development of Water bodies
- Community Rain Water Harvesting Projects
- Appropriate pricing of Water to discourage wastage.

Sustainable water means a nation that can be water self-sufficient: ensuring there is enough water to meet multiple needs, from agriculture to municipal and industrial. It also means water supply will remain consistent, despite climate change impacts, such as a lack of rainfall and drought, or too much rain and being flood resilient. Sustainable water also means that the economics stack up in matching supply and demand and the water delivery process is as efficient as possible. Water sustainability, meanwhile, can also mean energy neutrality by coupling traditional water treatment technologies with renewable energies.

13.1 What is Water Sustainability?

Sustainable water management means the ability to meet the water needs of the present without compromising the ability of future generations to do the same. Achieving sustainable water management requires a multidisciplinary and holistic approach in which technical, environmental, economic, landscape aesthetic, societal and cultural issues are addressed.

On a global scale, having sustainable water means to provide each person on the planet with affordable access to the minimum 20 to 50 litres of daily water required to sustain life. This follows the United Nations General Assembly recognition of "the right to safe and cleaning drinking water and sanitation as a human right that is essential for the full enjoyment of life and all human rights".

Water sustainability also means effective and holistic management of water resources. There are now multiple demands on water resources, which drive the need for sustainable, integrated and holistic water management.

Water is used:

1. for drinking as a survival necessity,
2. in industrial operations (energy production, manufacturing of goods, etc.),
3. for domestic applications (cooking, cleaning, bathing, sanitation), and
4. agriculture.

Sustainable water supply is a component of integrated water resource management, the practice of bringing together multiple stakeholders with various viewpoints in order to determine how water should best be managed.

A water supply system will be sustainable only if it promotes efficiencies in both the supply and the demand sides. Initiatives to meet demand for water supply will be sustainable if they prioritize measures to avoid water waste. Avoiding wastage will contribute to reducing water consumption and, consequently, to delaying the need for new resources.

On the supply side, it is fundamental to enhance operation and maintenance capabilities of water utilities, reducing non-revenue water (NRW), leakages, and energy use, as well as improving the capacity of the workforce to understand and operate the system. It is also necessary to ensure cost-recovery through a fair tariff system and "intelligent" investment planning. In addition, all alternatives to increase the water supply must be analysed considering the entire life cycle.

On the demand side, the adoption of water efficient technology can considerably reduce water consumption. Investments in less water intensive industrial processes and more efficient buildings lead to a more sustainable water supply. Concrete possibilities of economic savings, social benefits (such as the involvement of different sectors of society to reach a common objective, environmental awareness of the population, etc.) and a range of environmental gains make the adoption of water efficient technologies viable.

Sustainable water supply involves a sequence of combined actions and not isolated strategies. It depends on the individual's willingness to save water, governmental regulations, changes in the building industry, industrial processes reformulation, land occupation, etc. The challenge is to create mechanisms of regulation, incentives and affordability to ensure the sustainability of the system.

13.2 Water, Energy and Food Security Nexus

The water, energy and food security nexus according to the Food And Agriculture Organisation of the United Nations (FAO), means that water security, energy security and food security are very much linked to one another, meaning that the actions in any one particular area often can have effects in one or both of the other areas.

These three sectors (water, energy and food security nexus) are necessary for the benefit of human well-being, poverty reduction and sustainable development. As the world population is nearing 8 billion, increasing demands for basic services also rise, such as the growing desires for higher living standards and the need for more conscious stewardship of the vital resources required to achieve those services and these desires have become both more obvious and urgent.

Water-food-energy connections lie at the heart of sustainable, economic and environmental development and protection. The demand for all three resources continues to grow for various reasons: a growing population, ongoing population movements from farms to cities, rising incomes, increased desire to spend those incomes on energy and water intensive goods/varying diets, international trade, urbanization and climate change. Water being a finite resource, but also the most abundant resource of the three sectors is the most exploited. Water is primarily used in forestry and fishery, agricultural production (in its entire agri-food supply chain) and is used to create and/or transfer energy in varying forms. In fact, agriculture is the largest user of freshwater, making it responsible for 70% of total global withdrawal, while more than one fourth of energy used worldwide is an input for food production, distribution, and use.

In addition, food production and supply chain simultaneously utilize approximately 30% of the total energy that is used globally. The greater the capacity to pay for improved water, the more it will enable alternative water sources, such as desalination to bring water into urban areas from greater distances, such as desalinated seawater often requiring energy-intensive production and transport methods.

Countries, food, water and energy industries, as well as other users can agree that the increasing use of more water, energy and land resources (food) have a great potential to face issues with environmental deterioration and even resource scarcity, as we can already see taking place in some parts of the developing world. The unbroken links between these sectors continues to demand well-integrated plans to protect food and water and food security.

13.2.1 Interactions among the water, energy and food security sectors

The interactions among water, energy and food are numerous and substantial. Water is used for extraction, mining, processing, refining, and residue disposal of fossil fuels, as well as for growing feedstock for biofuels and for generating electricity. Water intensity varies in the energy sector, with oil and gas production requiring much less water than oil from tar sands or biofuels. Choosing biofuels for energy production should require a careful balancing of priorities, since water that has been used to grow feedstock for biofuels could also have been used to grow food.

Many forms of energy production through fossil fuels are highly polluting in addition to being water intensive, especially extraction from tar sands and shale and extraction through hydraulic fracturing. Further, return flows from power plants to rivers are warmer than the water that was taken in and/or are highly polluted and can consequently compromise other downstream usage, including ecosystems. Conversely, energy is needed for extracting, transporting, distributing and treating water. Energy intensity for accessing a cubic meter of water varies: logically, accessing local surface water requires far less energy than pumping groundwater, reclaiming wastewater or desalinating seawater. Irrigation is more energy intensive than rain-fed agriculture, and drip irrigation is more intensive yet since the water must be pressurized.

Food production is by far the largest consumer of global fresh water supplies. Globally, agriculture is responsible for an average of 70% of fresh water consumption by humans; in some countries that figure jumps to 80%-90%. Agriculture is therefore also responsible for much of fresh water over-exploitation. Food production further impacts the water sector through land degradation, changes in runoff, disruption of groundwater discharge, water quality and availability of water and land for other purposes such as natural habitat. The increased yields that have resulted from mechanization and other modern measures have come at a high energy price, as the full food and supply chain claims approximately 30% of total global energy demand.

Energy fuels land preparation, fertilizer production, irrigation and the sowing, harvesting and transportation of crops. The links between food and energy have become quite apparent in recent years as increases in the price of oil lead very quickly to increases in the price of food. The energy sector can have other negative impacts on the food sector when mining for fossil fuels and deforestation for biofuels reduce land for agriculture, ecosystems and other uses.

13.2.2 Nexus approach

Improved water, energy, and food security on a global level can be achieved through a nexus approach—an approach that integrates management and governance across sectors and scales. A nexus approach can support the transition to a Sustainable Economy, which aims, among other things, at resource use efficiency and greater policy coherence. Given the increasing interconnectedness across sectors and in space and time, a reduction of negative economic, social and environmental externalities can increase overall resource use efficiency, provide additional benefits and secure the human rights to water and food. In a nexus-based approach, conventional policy- and decision-making in "silos" therefore would give way to an approach that reduces trade-offs and builds synergies across sectors. The European Union, working along with the German Federal Ministry for Economics Cooperation and Development and the International Food Policy Research Institute, the WWF and the World Economic Forum have developed an online resource on this concern. Nexus approach requires an integrated solution.

13.2.3 Nexus perspective

A nexus perspective increases the understanding of the interdependencies across the water, energy and food sectors and influences policies in other areas of concern such as climate and biodiversity. The nexus perspective helps to move beyond silos and ivory towers that preclude interdisciplinary solutions, thus increasing opportunities for mutually beneficial responses and enhancing the potential for cooperation between and among all sectors. Everyone in all disciplines needs to think and act from the perspective of being interlinked in order to realize the full impact of both direct and indirect synergies that can result.

A deep understanding of the nexus will provide the informed and transparent framework that is required to meet increasing global demands without compromising sustainability. The nexus approach will also allow decision-makers to develop appropriate policies, strategies and investments, to explore and exploit synergies, and to identify and mitigate trade-offs among the development goals related to water, energy and food security. Active participation by and among government agencies, the private sector and civil society is critical to avoiding unintended adverse consequences. A true nexus approach can only be achieved through close collaboration of all actors from all sectors.

While the opportunities provided by the nexus perspective and the consequent social, environmental and economic benefits are real, implementation requires the right policies, incentives and encouragement, and institutions and leaders that are up to the task, as well as frameworks that encourage empowerment, research, information and education. Accelerating the involvement of the private sector through establishing and promoting the business case for both sustainability and the nexus is essential to driving change and getting to scale.

13.3 Water Supply Sources

13.3.1 Surface water

Surface freshwater is unfortunately limited and unequally distributed in the world. In addition, pollution from various activities leads to surface water that is not drinking quality. Therefore, treatment systems (either large scale or at the household level) must be put in place.

Structures such as dams may be used to impound water for consumption. Dams can be used for power generation, water supply, irrigation, flood prevention, water diversion, navigation, etc. If properly designed and constructed, dams can help provide a sustainable water supply. The design should consider peak flood flows (historical and projected for climate change), earthquake faults, soil permeability, slope stability and erosion, silting, wetlands, water table, human impacts, ecological impacts (including wildlife), compensation for resettlement, and other site characteristics. There are various challenges that large-scale dam projects may present to sustainability: negative environmental impacts on wildlife habitats, fish migration, water flow and quality, and socioeconomic impacts resulting from resettled local communities. A sustainability impact assessment should therefore be performed to determine the environmental, economic and social consequences of the construction.

13.3.2 Groundwater

Groundwater accounts for greater than 50% of global freshwater; thus, it is critical for potable water. Groundwater can be a sustainable water supply source if the total amount of water entering, leaving, and being stored in the system is conserved. There are three main factors which determine the source and amount of water flowing through a groundwater system: precipitation, location of streams and other surface-water bodies, and evapotranspiration rate; it is thus not possible to generalize a sustainable withdrawal or pumping rate for groundwater.

Unsustainable groundwater use results in water-level decline, reduced stream flow, and low water quality, jeopardizing the livelihood of effected communities. Various practices of sustainable groundwater supply include changing rates or spatial patterns of ground-water pumpage, increasing recharge to the ground-water system, decreasing discharge from the groundwater system, and changing the volume of groundwater in storage at different time scales. A long-term vision is necessary when extracting groundwater since the effects of its development can take years before becoming apparent. It is important to integrate groundwater supply within adequate land planning and sustainable urban drainage systems.

13.3.3 Rainwater Harvesting

Collecting water from precipitation is one of the most sustainable sources of water supply since it has inherent barriers to the risk of over-exploitation found in surface and groundwater sources, and directly provides drinking water quality. However, rainwater harvesting systems must be properly designed and maintained in order to collect water efficiently, prevent contamination and use sustainable treatment systems in case the water is contaminated. A number of drinking water treatments exist at point-of-use, each with advantages and disadvantages. These include solar treatment, boiling, using filters, chlorination, combined methods such as filtration and chlorination, flocculation and chlorination. Although technically given the Earth's surface and precipitation, rainwater harvesting can meet global water demand, the solution can most practically be a supplement to sustainable water supply systems given a level of uncertainty (especially with climate change), and competing land-use applications.

13.3 4 Reclaimed Water

Reclaimed water, or water recycled from human use, can also be a sustainable source of water supply. It is an important solution to reduce stress on primary water resources such as surface and groundwater. There are both centralized and decentralized systems which include grey water recycling systems and the use of microporous membranes. Reclaimed water must be treated to provide the appropriate quality for a given application (irrigation, industry use, etc.). It is often most efficient to separate grey water from black water, thereby using the two water streams for different uses. Grey water comes from domestic activities such as washing, whereas black water contains human waste. The characteristics of the two waste streams thus differ.

13.3.5 Desalinization

Desalinisation has the potential to provide an adequate water quantity to those regions that are freshwater poor, including small island states. However, the energy demands of reverse osmosis, a widely-used procedure used to remove salt from water, are a challenge to the adaptation of this technology as a sustainable one. The costs of desalination average around 0.81 USD per cubic meter compared to roughly 0.16 USD per cubic meter from other supply sources (USGS, 2010). If desalination can be provided with renewable energies and efficient technologies, the sustainable features of this supply source would increase. Currently, desalination increases operational costs because of the needed energy (and also carbon dioxide emissions); this in turn raises the cost of the final product. In addition, desalination plants can have negative impacts on marine life, and cause water pollution due to the chemicals used to treat water and the discharge of brine.

13.3.6 Bottled Water

Bottled water is a 21st century phenomenon whereby mostly private companies provide potable water in a bottle for a cost. In some areas, bottled water is the only reliable source of safe drinking water. However, often in these same locations, the cost is prohibitively expensive for the local population to use in a sustainable manner. Bottled water is not considered an "improved drinking water source" when it is the only potable source available. When sustainability metrics are used to access bottled water, it falls short in many situations of being a sustainable water supply. Economic costs, pollution associated with its manufacturing (plastic, energy, etc.) and transportation, as well as extra water use, makes bottled water an unsustainable water supply system for many regions and for many brands. It takes 3-4 liters of water to make less than 1 liter of bottled water.

13.4 Water Uses

13.4.1 Water in Agriculture

Agriculture uses the largest amount of freshwater on a global scale. It represents roughly 70% of all water withdrawal worldwide, with various regional differences. In the United

States, for example, agriculture accounts for over 80% of water consumption.

The productivity of irrigated land is approximately three times greater than that of rain-fed land. Thus, irrigation is an important factor for sustainable agriculture systems. Agriculture is also responsible for some of the surface and groundwater degradation because of run-off (chemical and erosion-based). It thus has a dual role in sustainable water supply:

1. using water efficiently for irrigation and
2. protecting surface and groundwater supply sources.

Techniques for sustainable water supply in agriculture include organic farming practices which limit substances that would contaminate water, efficient water delivery, micro-irrigation systems, adapted water lifting technologies, zero tillage, rainwater harvesting, runoff farming, and drip irrigation (efficient method that allows water to drip slowly to plant roots by using pipes, valves, tubes and emitters).

13.4.2 Water in Industry

Water is used in just about every industry. Industrial water withdrawals represent 22% of total global water use (significant regional differences). Its use is notable for manufacturing, processing, washing, diluting, cooling, transporting substances, sanitation needs within a facility, incorporating water into a final product, etc. The food, paper, chemicals, refined petroleum, and primary metal industries use large amounts of water.

A sustainable water supply in industry involves limiting water use through efficient appliances and methods adapted to the particular industry. Rainwater harvesting on-site (including the creation of large pond-like structures), as well as recycling water in industrial processes, can provide a sustainable water supply for industry without straining municipal water supplies. Industry releases organic water pollutants, heavy metals, solvents, toxic sludge, and other wastes into water supply sources. Industry thus has a dual responsibility for internal sustainable water supply and the protection of external water supply sources.

13.4. 3 Domestic Water Uses

Potable water requires some of the strictest standards of quality in terms of bacteriological and chemical pollutants. These standards are often governed by national governments; international recommendations can be found from the World Health Organization

(https://apps.who.int/iris/bitstream/handle/10665/254637/9789241549950-eng.pdf?sequence=1).

Drinking water must be fresh water and should be free of pathogens and free of harmful chemicals.

The average household needs an estimated 20-50 liters of water per person per day, depending on various assumptions and practices. Reducing water use through waterless toilets, water efficient appliances, and water quantity monitoring, is an important part of sustainability for domestic water supply. Efficient piping systems that are leak-free and well insulated provide a network that is reliable and help to limit water waste. The aforementioned potable water supply sources, with their sustainability features and sustainability challenges, are all relevant to other domestic uses. Since water quality standards are not as strict for household uses as for drinking, there is more flexibility when considering sustainable domestic water supply (including the potential for reclaimed water use).

13.5 Water Pyramid Approach

Similar to "Energy Pyramid Approach", The Mission suggests a Water Pyramid as depicted in Fig-3 for optimum use of water.

13.5.1 Water Conservation Techniques/ideas

1. Zero Leakage – Replace leaking taps immediately.
2. Start with yourself. Measure the daily water that you use and try to reduce the amount.
3. Examine the usage pattern of water in your family or in any one family. Educate them to use water with more care and efficiency.
4. Reuse Water
    - Water used for cleaning vegetables for Gardening purposes
    - Water used for washing clothes for floor/car cleaning.
    - If possible store water after bath and use it for cooling roof in summer or just spread it on the dusty roads to reduce pollution.
5. Don't keep the water running while using the washbasin.
6. In wash basins, replace ordinary taps with self-closing taps. Or, remove the taps and keep a bucket of water with a mug.
7. Install shower outlet for kitchen tap. It will reduce the amount of water used for cleaning utensils.

8. Take quick showers instead of baths or take a sponge bath instead of a shower.
9. Use only low-volume and dual flush toilets. If you still have an old type of Cistern Insert old water bottle inside it to reduce the water volume.
10. Buy a front-loading washing machine. It uses 40 % less water than the top-loading one.
11. Run dishwashers or washing machines only with full loads.
12. Clean your Car with just 1 Litre of water by using a spray can.
13. Use drip irrigation for your garden. Water after dusk.
14. Replace lawns by trees and shrubs that need little fertilizer and are drought-resistant. Or, grow vegetables.
15. Grow only those plants that require low amounts of water.
16. Use liberal amounts of mulch to reduce water evaporation.
17. Implement rainwater harvesting in your house or apartment block.
18. Collect condensate water from Air-conditioner.
19. Get together with your neighbours and other city residents to start regular meetings to learn about how the rainwater and the city's piped water supply work in your city and become water literate so you can spread the water literacy in forums and networks you are active in.

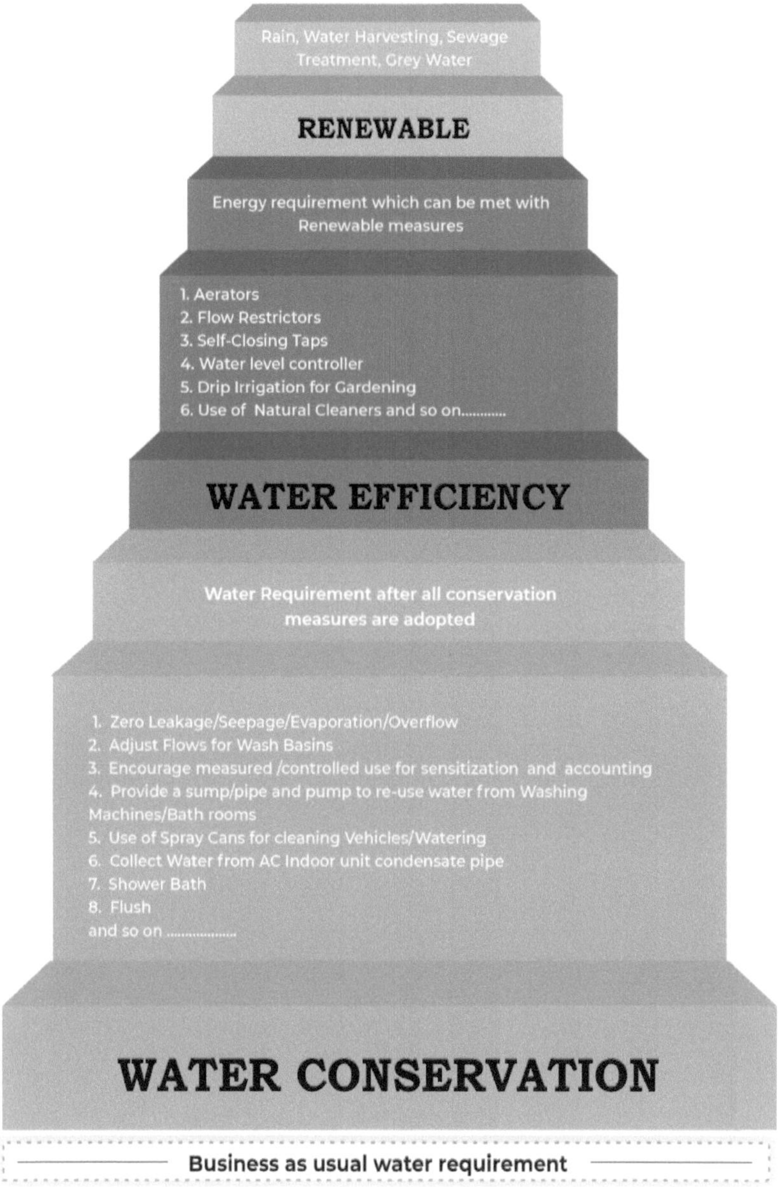

Sustainable Water Management Pyramid

Fig-3

14

Sustainable Transportation

Highlights:

- Importance of transport and its various forms.
- Impacts of transport on society, economy, and our environment.
- Key considerations and strategies for sustainable transport.
- Solutions to enhance people health, prosperity and planet

14.0 Introduction

Mobility is inherent to nature, and significant for the survival of a specie. All creatures including humans have the ability to move on their own. But the homo sapiens stole a march over all others using their ability to innovate. The invention of wheel brought about a revolutionary change in the way humans moved and migrated from one place to another. They needed to move to different places first in search of food, shelter, better climes, and then as their feudal instincts developed, they had to travel to conquer other territories and widen their fiefdom. Initially, the wanderers walked and traversed large distances, but as they started domesticating animals, horse, elephants, oxen, sheep, and dogs were roped in to pull carts and sledges.

The second revolution came with the invention of steam engine. The possibility of a motorized transport changed the transportation scenario globally, and from then on saw exponential growth in transport systems.

Humans remained in incessant search for faster and more efficient ways to travel, and continue to do so even today, as they now aspire to travel beyond this planet. This quest for travel is not only borne out of a need for economic growth of the human race, but now it is also adventurism, exploration, sport and leisure. Transportation of goods and people is the greatest enabler, rather the backbone of economic development. In the Indian context, transportation contributes 6.3% of our GDP.

14.1 Types of Transportation Systems

Types of transport refer to a combination of networks, infrastructures, types of vehicles, and operations, be it on land, or water, or in space. These include walking, road transport, rail, marine and modern aviation. There would be variations within each of these modes of transportation systems which have emerged over time, but essentially there are five (5) modes of transportation systems which are listed below.

1. Road transport
2. Railway transport
3. Water transport
4. Air transport
5. Pipeline transport

14.1.1 Road transport

Road transport is the most common, most used, and exists in all parts of the world in various forms. Motorised transport includes automobiles, trucks, buses, scooters, motor-cycles, and all such vehicles that are powered by fossil fuel driven engines, or electric motors (now). Simpler, non-powered vehicles are pedal operated bicycles. All of these vehicles move on specific terrestrial tracks referred to as roads which could be concrete, tarred, paved or mud tracks.

Road transport, when compared with other modes of transportation, is relatively flexible, cheaper and faster. This mode has a high capacity for carrying goods over short distances. But these advantages appear miniscule in comparison to the enormous vehicular pollution and emission of GHGs due to combustion of fossil fuels. which today is the single issue hammering the sustainability of our planet. Besides this major disadvantage, maintenance of roads and infrastructure are some drawbacks with this mode of transport.

14.1.2 Rail transport

Railways were developed during the period of the industrial revolution in the 19th century. Development of railways in many countries was achieved to serve both, political and economic objectives of rulers. Railways when compared to any mode of transport on land, are the cheapest to operate, and contribute least to pollution and GHG emissions. Other major advantages of railway transport include reliability, ability to convey heavy and bulky goods, over any distance, economic, safe, and also comfortable for passengers. The development of infrastructure however, calls for heavy initial investments.

14.1.3 Water transport

Water transport is very important because it is the cheapest way of transporting bulky goods and people over long distances on rivers and oceans. There are two major types of water transport namely, (a) Inland water transport and (b) Sea water transport (maritime).

14.1.3.1 Inland Water transport

This is the system of transport through all navigable rivers, lakes, and man-made canals. Many large rivers in different parts of the world are used by ships and barges for transportation; the main rivers where inland water transport is important are the Rhine and Danube in Europe, Zaire in Africa, the Nile in Africa, the Mississippi in the USA, etc.

14.1.3.2 Maritime (Shipping) Water transport

However, Ocean waterways carry a lot of the world's trade, the majority of the bulky goods, materials, and passengers pass through ocean waterways from one country to another at the cheapest cost.

14.1.4 Air Transport (Aviation)

Air transport is the fastest means of transport, and it is for this reason that aviation industry has seen stupendous growth since inception. This mode of transportation provides both domestic and international connectivity for transporting human beings and goods. Air transport incidentally has the maximum contribution to carbon footprint with short-haul flights being the worst contributors when measured on per passenger per km basis.

14.1.5 Pipeline transport

This system of transportation involves pumping of liquids and gaseous items such as water, crude oil, petroleum/diesel, and gas through hollow pipes. of. Here again, the transfer of these goods can take place within the country on internationally. This mode is easily monitored for safety and reliability, and scores over alternative means of tankers which add to GHG emissions.

14.1.6 Other modes of transportation

14.1.6.1 Animal-powered transport

Is the oldest means of transportation, involving use of animals for transportation of people and goods. Humans may ride some of the animals (camels, horses, donkeys, elephants, etc.) or harness them to pull carts and buggies. which is mostly referred to as a beast of burden.

14.1.6.2 Human-powered transport

Is the most omnipresent form of transport, which engages people, goods or both to move from one place to another using human muscle -power – this will include walking, running and swimming. Modern technology has however allowed machines (eg., a bicycle) to enhance this human power to achieve speed and efficiency. This form is popular for reasons of cost-saving, physical exercise, leisure, and environmentalism. In underdeveloped regions, this may perhaps be the only form of transport available.

14.1.6.3 Spaceflight

Spacecraft transport, as of now is reserved for exploratory travel beyond the Earth's atmosphere into outer space. It is also utilised to put satellites into orbit and conduct scientific experiments. Space travel involves huge resources with intensive R&D. Hitherto, this was primarily in the domains of developed nations only, but private enterprise has also begun to make inroads into space travel.

14.1.6.4 Cable transport

Also termed as conveyor transport, or ropeways, enables movement of goods and passengers to be moved on cable trollies or cars pulled by motors. These are not so common and generally preferred to connect two points straddling a valley or a river, where road transport would be rather difficult and time taking. Use of pulleys and balancing of loads going up and down are common elements of cable transport. These could also include escalators, lifts, etc.

14.2 Impact of Transportation on the Planet and People

While on one hand, the contribution of transport sector in any developed or developing economy cannot be denigrated, the flip side too cannot be ignored. Transportation sector is responsible for 28% of the total global energy consumption, and 64% of the total oil consumption, in 2020. Commensurately, transport sector accounted for 24% of direct CO2 emission from fuel consumption, globally. Of this, road transport share is more than 12%, but in India, the road transport alone contributes a whopping 87% of our total GHG emission from this sector. This is evident from the fact that fossil fuels are the main energy source powering transportation systems in our country, thus making a phenomenal contribution to both, pollution and GHG emission.

Thus, the need to plan for sustainable transport is imminent. The impacts of global warming are now known and being felt by every being on the planet. There are plenty of tell-tale signs forewarning us of the dangers.

About 400 polluting compounds are emitted by petrol and diesel vehicles and from petrol vapor, which directly and indirectly impact our Planet and People, their health, economy, and prosperity.

14.3 Concepts of Sustainable Transportation

"The goal of sustainable transportation is to ensure that transportation is inclusive, affordable, accessible, resilient, adaptable and safe making positive social, environmental and economic impacts. Sustainable transport should be logistics and transit oriented, multi-modal with synergy between all modes.

A sustainable transportation system shall imply provision of services and infrastructure for the mobility of people and goods for advancing their economic and social development such that "fossil fuel consumption, vehicle emissions, safety, congestion, and social and economic access are of such levels that they can be sustained into the indefinite future without causing great or irreparable harm to future generations of people throughout the world." The use of energy shall be affordable, accessible, efficient, and resilient, with zero or minimum carbon and other emissions and environmental impacts.

The three key pillars of sustainable transportation are:

1. Inclusiveness: Safe, affordable, with good mobility, and accessible to all sections of the society, including the

disadvantaged (blind, on wheelchair, senior citizens, children, etc.)

2. Resilience: Robust, capacity to resist and absorb disruptions, and ability to recover from disruptions to normal/designed operational levels (eg., cyclones, floods, disasters, war, etc.)
3. Sustainability: Least negative impact on environment, least emissions. It should identify with and go beyond achieving the 17 SDGs.

Futuristic modes of transport system shall be diverse and multi-modal. This generally means integration of walking, cycling, ride-sharing, public transit, car-pooling, telework and local delivery services, so as to create more walkable and transit-oriented communities.

Use of any emerging technology should be evaluated on the basis of its' Life Cycle Assessment". Eg., impact of rapid charging battery manufacturing, disposal and recycling, on our ecology needs a deeper study.

14.3.1 Sustainable Transportation Objectives and its effect:

14.3.1.1 Transport activity objectives with indicators:

- ✓ Decrease personalised motor vehicle transport and increase use of more sustainable rapid public transport modes; Decongest mega cities; Develop infrastructure - multi-level bridges, bicycle lanes, through fares, etc.
  Indicators: Vehicle/Passenger- km per capita.
- ✓ Decrease energy consumption through improved and efficient combustion; increased use of bio and eco-friendly

fuels; reduced tare weight of vehicles; Introduction of aerofoil designs to reduce drag, etc.
Indicators: Total/Per capita energy consumption as per mode and fuel.

✓ Decrease GHG emissions by encouraging mass transportation; Augmenting water and sea ways, bicycling and walking lanes; Development and usage of eco-friendly fuels like hydrogen and bio fuels; Use of Google maps for alerts on traffic congestion, shortest routes, etc.
Indicators: GHG emissions by mode of transport per km-per capita

14.3.1.2 Social Activity

✓ Decrease space taken by transport facilities; Change in land use for multi-level roads, generating bicycle and walking lanes, parks, etc.
Indicators: Distribution of population, dwellings, total land area served by cars-per capita;

✓ Access to basic services - Percentage of population commuting to work, by mode, trip origin and destination.
Indicators: Access to public transit (road/rail) within 1 - 2 Km distance; Percentage of population living within 500m of transit station, or living within Metro Transit's service area; Number of Metro transit passengers using ferries and conventional buses.

14.3.1.3 Economic Activity

✓ Decrease personal expenditure on transportation by improving system energy efficiency; Share savings with people; Lower cost of renewable energy sources/fuels;
Indicators: Expenditure on personal mobility; Percentage of household expenditure spent on transportation.

14.3.2 Personal transportation places excessive demand on parking space requiring unproductive land use, idling of vehicles resulting in vehicular tail-pipe emissions, with traffic congestions further adding to this misery. Number of vehicles in India is doubling every 8-10 years.

Comparison of common urban modes of transport based on CO_2 emitted per passenger-per kM reveals rail transportation to be most favourable to the environment:

Rail	14
Small automobile	42
Average automobile	55
Bus	68
Two-wheeler	72
Airplane	285

This puts emphasis on greater utilization of mass transportation modes. These unlock space making it available for green parks, public spaces that invoke lifestyle community benefits and social cohesion. There is less of stress, road accidents, trauma. About 1.2 lakh people die in road accidents every year. Civic amenities for elderly, children, disabled, women are more easily achieved.

Land use & transport policies shape urban growth as energy "trim" not "obese" by redistributing road space. The most sustainable strategies are those that simultaneously help achieve most of these objectives. These strategies may include alternative modes of transportation (electric vehicles - charged through renewable sources, hydrogen fuel powered vehicles, metros, and waterways) and fuels (solar, nuclear, hydrogen, natural gas, bio fuels, synthetic fuel, fuel cells), lightweight materials in manufacturing vehicles, etc.

14.4 Important Key Considerations/Strategies for Sustainable Transportation Planning

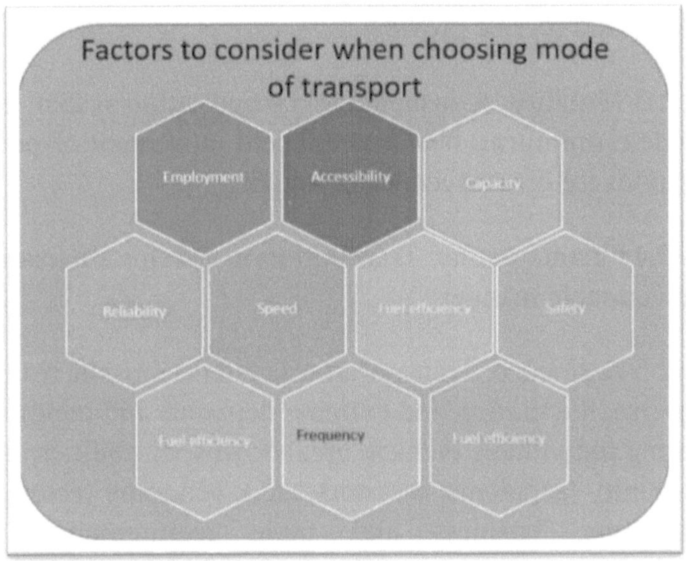

14.4.1 Salient key considerations: safety, accessibility, equity & equal mobility, system efficiency, security, prosperity, economic viability, eco-friendly, least waste generation whole transport, resource consumption, net emissions. User has a plethora of options to choose from.

Various modes and components of the transport system are to be well integrated to provide free flowing movement, last mile connectivity with efficient land use planning. Factors that need consideration include:

14.4.2.1 Affordability: Affordable transport options must provide access to lower-income households and daily workplace commuter. This shall factor in pricing, parking, insurance and fuel.

14.4.2.2 Land use accessibility to achieve smart growth will have policies to support mixed, connected, multi-modal land use development, managing operational efficiency, transport agencies and service providers.

14.4.2.3 Mobility: A sustainable transportation system must provide economical, fast, and efficient movement of people and goods for greater economic activity.

14.4.2.4 Finance equity: Transportation systems are financed in an equitable manner.

14.4.2.5 Resilience: Transportation systems must be resilient to diverse, fluctuating and extreme demands and conditions affecting individuals (vehicle breakdowns, disabilities, etc.), community (accidents, disasters, etc.), economy (economic fluctuations, business and trade requirements, fuel availability, etc.), strategy (future population growth rate, technological developments, etc.), and system design and capability (ability to handle and bounce back from extreme adversities).

14.4.2.6 Inclusivity: Sustainable transportation systems should address the concerns of physically disadvantaged sections of the society, such as people who are blind, on wheelchair, on crutches, senior citizens, etc. Easy, intuitive, enabling facilities – elevators, ramps, design barriers, spoken announcements for visually impaired. According to WHO, 15% of world's population lives with some form of disability, and 80% of this population resides in low-income countries.

14.4.2.7 Renewable fuel use: Hydrogen fuel based transportation has to be encouraged and made affordable.

Impact on environment during the process of manufacturing hydrogen fuel has to be considered and the changeover planned for quick and easy adaptability. Decarbonization, phasing out of Internal Combustion engines is the overall objective, but this may not happen soon.

Focus on renewable energy source especially solar is being driven recklessly. Manufacturing of solar PV panels, their efficient operation, disposal after enhanced life and recycling issues have to be holistically reviewed to assess net GHG emission levels.

14.4.2.8 Technological interventions: Technological upgradations are required to remove inefficiencies in existing transportation systems due to poorly maintained road, heavily congested roads and traffic, quality of fossil fuel - content of sulphur, trace toxic chemicals, and their polluting potential. Thrust on development of new 3rd & 4th generation bio fuels from algae, etc., shall have to be given.

Adoption of low carbon, low emissions transport technologies like water ways, which have almost 60% less impact than road transport on per passenger-km basis, electrified rail systems, etc., shall have to be prioritized in national policies.

14.4.3 Thus, serious planning, liberal budget allocations and committed R&D shall have to be marshalled for sustainable transportation of people in the Planet, ensuring peace, safety, and prosperity globally.

Planning has to be comprehensive integrating all major objectives, impacts and options. Decision-making shall be coordinated among different sectors, jurisdictions and agencies, and include participation of all stakeholders.

The excessive commuting hours are a precious time lost by people which could have been spent with family, in self-development and wellness enhancement activities. Much of these problems could be averted by setting up residences near the workplace. Same logic of minimizing travel time becomes applicable to educational institutes. In USA and many European countries, the school admission criteria factors in the distance between the student's residence and school.

Pooling or sharing of vehicles, availability and use of rapid mass transit systems like buses, metro trains, MLVs, digitalization of information on these facilities, schedules, and integration of mobile applications help to reduce the carbon footprint and encourage sustainability while maintaining convenience for the masses. Penalties be imposed if a vehicle is used just for travel of one person, without valid reasons.

Service roads, pavements, pedestrians' paths all have to be kept free from encroachment by hawkers and vendors, as is typically seen in our cities and towns. Encroachments choke the traffic resulting in increased tail-pipe emissions. Many towns have now barred vehicle entry during peak hour rush in busy market areas.

14.4.4 Accidents are a bane of any society. Accidents in transportation sector are a direct outcome of improper and inadequate infrastructure, negligence, traffic congestion, laxity in laws and compliances. With 1.2 lakh on-road accidental deaths, it is a huge cost to our national economy besides pain and penury to the family of victims. In Mumbai and Bengaluru, several people have died just driving over potholes on roads. Drunken driving and running over of pedestrians and bicyclists is a common news in our country. Snail paced and idling traffic directly impacts fuel consumption besides adding to the severity of adverse health impacts due to pollution, and GHG emissions leading to climate change.

Stringent tests for vehicle drivers, vehicle fitness checks, and pollution certificates have to be rigorously enforced. This will also assist in reducing road accidents and make travelling safer. Penalties for law violation have to be made severe and harsher. Repeat violations must invoke permanent cancellation of license.

Use of IoT, AI, ML, GPS, and all forms of digitalization and communication techniques by deploying CCTVs for monitoring traffic, monitoring of pollution levels, providing diversion and rerouting advisory for decongesting thoroughfares for speedy transit, booking of driving and traffic offenders, providing emergency assistance to needy, contributes to People, Prosperity and Peace.

14.4.5 Our country has been gifted with a very long coastline of more than 7,500 KMs. In addition, we have 14,000 KMs of canal & riverways network that could provide unrestricted transit waterway passage. This opens up opportunities for augmenting these waterways for mass and goods transportation which will drastically reduce pressure on road and rail networks, lower dependency on fossil fuels, and in turn reduce carbon emissions.

14.4.6 Road widening and development of multi-lanes is often not an environment friendly method to decongest traffic. It leads to greater urbanisation. Additional urban space requirements pushes the boundaries into countryside agriculture fields, which in turn get pushed into forests areas resulting in their destruction. Moving vertically upwards by constructing over bridges, and multi-tiered roads - one over another, appears a better proposition.

Hassle free transit systems promote tourism. Providing litter free, emission free public and civic amenities at regular distances with high frequency connections, will boost tourism. Thailand, Sri Lanka are known to have exploited their tourism potential to great advantage. Develop and incentivise bicycle usage culture like in many European countries by providing dedicated lanes.

14.4.7 'One Family-One Vehicle Policy': Is it possible to implement this? This would be a rather stringent diktat that can percolate down from an autocratic authority only. The rich can avoid dropping their children at school in their own vehicles. On the contrary educate and 'prepare' them to use school van, which will discourage snobbery and inequality, leading to harmony within the society. Further encouragement is possible by favourably ranking students in their eco-grading when they comply.

14.4.8 Home Office/Work from home: Many businesses, essentially in the IT sector, call-centre offices, and several other advisory services, do not really necessitate employees to sit cocooned at one place called an office. This phenomenon stands well tested during the two years of pandemic. Commuting hours were more gainfully utilized. Office space and several other ancillary requirements for operating an office were dispensed with. The resultant reduction in traffic, energy requirements of offices, and pollution, Home office should be mandated wherever possible. It is a win-win situation for employer and employee and complements towards sustainable family and transportation

14.5 Performance Indicators for Measurement of Sustainable Transportation

Economic productivity & development, energy efficiency, affordability, operational efficiency, de- congestion, commuting time reduction, fairness in pricing, safety and reliability, usage friendly for partially abled and senior citizens.

Per capita GDP, share of transportation in the budget, per-capita congestion delay, losses due to congestion; efficient pricing (road, parking, insurance, fuel, etc.), per capita traffic casualty (injury and death) rates; traveller assault (crime) rates;

Heritage protection, climate stability, air, water and noise pollution;

Per capita emissions of GHGs, VOCs, PM, NOx, etc., Air quality standards and management's pollution containment plans; Noise level audit results; Frequency of air pollution standard violations; Reduced marine oil spills and damage to coral reefs and protection of fisheries.

Open space preservation, good planning and efficient pricing:

Per capita land devoted to transport facilities; Portion of population engaged in planning decisions.

Range of objectives, impacts and options considered. · Efficient and equitable funding allocation, Measurement of performance Indicators with good governance on sustainable transportation and sure will benefits the Citizens.

Resilience metrics include robustness, redundancy, resourcefulness, and rapidity of mobilization.

14.6 The Way Forward

14.6.1 Expectations of citizens from the Ministry of Surface/ Sea/Air Transportation by implementing Sustainable Transportation:

- ✓ Improvement in the transport networks, frequency of services & quality of transport – both in urban and rural areas; Better roads, express ways,
- ✓ Increase in productivity, energy and economic efficiency in all modes of transport
- ✓ Enhancement in civic amenities and comfort levels; Provision of facilities for the disadvantaged persons, children and senior citizens; Making cities more humane and liveable;
- ✓ Address the problem of pollution – monitor and control, Improving the environment quality;
- ✓ Reduce noise pollution; Stop degradation of environment and landscape;
- ✓ Increased mobility for all; Providing last mile connectivity; Rapid transit systems such that these discourage use of personal vehicles;
- ✓ Disciplining traffic; Reduction in accidents and death rates; Better safety;
- ✓ Improved customer service; customized transportation requirements
- ✓ Thrust on long haul transportation by air, land and sea;
- ✓ Multi modal transport and supply chain management;
- ✓ Terminal management & logistic service providers to manage supply chains; Faster Turnaround of vessels, containers, wagons, trucks.

- ✓ Globalization, regional links, global trade and economy.
- ✓ A web-based society that may reduce travel for business and work; Encourage "work from home" culture wherever possible;
- ✓ Borderless transport across states with less or no proper work aided by IT; Removal of trade obstructions in transport planning and thinking;
- ✓ Maintenance of assets; Adaptation of new technology;
- ✓ Increased financial resources.
- ✓ Cost based pricing; Reduction, if not elimination, of subsidies.

14.6.2 Sensitizing Citizens

14.6.2.1 Promote public/mass transport:

Government/Private sector companies should provide some monetary incentive to employees who travel to office by walk, or bicycle, or public transport, or Company bus.

Parallel bicycling and pedestrian paths should be developed and maintained in all cities and towns.

14.6.2.2 Promote electric vehicles (EV) and charging stations with renewable sources:

Government itself is the largest user of vehicles for its humungous bureaucracy. It should mandate use of EVs in all departments, with solar powered charging stations built in all public spaces. Private organizations and industries can be asked to replicate similarly with charging facilities in their campus. All fuel filling stations should be asked to have at least one rooftop solar powered charging station.

14.6.2.3 Have a vehicle only if you have a parking space!

Parking of vehicles on the public road must be strictly banned. All gated communities and homes must mandatorily have garages and parking space. Penalty or rent should be collected if the vehicles are parked in public road/places. Creation of paid parking facilities for vehicles in the city and congested roads should be the norm, and the amount collected be utilized for providing better public services.

14.6.2.4 Compliance of traffic rules and regulations:

Ensure adherence of traffic rules and make vehicle fitness inspection stringent for all but must for public and school vans; Strict penalties, cancellation of license if offence is repeated, aided by technology (CCTV with auto registration plate reader, digital offence challan and fine booking, etc) will facilitate compliance and minimize corruption at the field level.

14.6.2.5 "Polluters to Pay" policy must be implemented: Vehicles with tail pipe emissions exceeding permissible limits should be taken off the road and owners penalised.

14.6.2.6 Sustainable transport is not possible unless cities are decongested.

Primarily, migration to cities has to be discouraged which can only be brought about by creating opportunities and avenues for people in education, employment, and recreation in rural areas and smaller towns. Expanding cities horizontally erodes into green belts creating further environmental problems. Astute planning to utilize existing space and infrastructure, and where expansion is must, making substantial provisions for forest & greenery to balance the development is required. This will also enable manage transportation without adding much to the carbon burden.

Locating institutional, commercial and industrial hubs has to be in a manner that does not allow build-up of traffic congestion. Flow of traffic through multi-modes with quick and easy connectivity near to place of work, residence, or study centre has to be incorporated in the planning and design. Instead of owned company vehicles, have chartered services which can be used as taxi/feeder bus and other purposes instead of being parked idle for most part of the day.

14.6.2.7 Use of physical separators on existing roads for demarcating bicycle and pedestrian lanes: Cycling must be encouraged. It not only improves Nation's Health Index, but also reduces our fuel bill and reduces pollution, besides decongesting roads and parking spaces.

A simple and cheap solution is to use old tyres, recycled plastic moulds, as separators, to avoid accidents.

14.6.2.8 Use of private vehicles and large multi-utility vehicles:

Egregious use of private vehicles for one person makes the current transportation system unsustainable. An empty seat in a moving vehicle is a wasted resource. The ever increasing automobile sales is generating various environmental, social and economic problems. Tail-pipe emissions of toxic and harmful substances is leading to unbearable levels of particulate matter concentration damaging human health, causing global warming, local air pollution, smog, disruptions of air and land traffic, etc.

While several technological interventions are being studied, analysed and tried to clean and reduce vehicular exhaust, economical solutions are as yet a distant dream. Preference for large fuel guzzling vehicles (SUVs and MUVs) thwarts any serious attempt to achieve sustainability. While the R&D departments of automobile manufacturers are ever trying to improve cut down on costs, improve vehicles' performance parameters in terms of distances per unit of fuel and reduced emissions, these benefits are eventually offset by the increased sales. The Jevons paradox - efficiency enables growth - comes into play here. Efficiency enables economic growth by allowing more to be produced from the same resources, but this enhanced economy also spurs consumption, nullifying the benefit derived from improved efficiency. This is the magic of industrial capitalism and the secret of growth. This puts onus on the behavior of individual car users.

14.6.2.9 Behavioral patterns of individuals impacts sustainable transportation:

- ✓ Adopt energy-efficient driving styles (e.g., drive at steady, optimum speed, timely shifting of gears);
- ✓ Type and size of vehicles used (eg., a large SUV for short journeys, or for a single person);
- ✓ Use car pools, public transport system; Use of digital apps (eg., quickride.in) have been found to be useful in commuting economically, without the need for your own vehicle;
- ✓ Adjust time of travel to avoid traffic jams and peak hour rush;

- ✓ Devote time and effort to keep vehicles well maintained and tuned for optimum fuel economy;
- ✓ Choose to have home and work place close by to reduce travelling distance and time.

14.6.2.10 Prioritizing sustainable transportation: It is essential to prioritize common and most used urban modes of transport in the following descending order in order to achieve sustainability:

1. Walking;
2. Bicycling;
3. Public transport – rail is best;
4. Taxis and shared vehicles;
5. Private Vehicle

14.7 Conclusion

Transportation can be achieved in a sustainable way when each and every citizen is sensitized to the ill effects of pollution, environmental and economic detriments of the use of fossil fuels. On the other hand, the several advantages of using mass transportation, bicycles for commuting, walking, etc., stand out. Awareness of the concerned authorities on improving the transport infrastructure, making it affordable, resilient, safe, and speedy, in conjunction with reduction in carbon footprint on the planet is essential. This will promote peace and prosperity of our citizens through their meaningful partnership.

15

Sustainable Manufacturing and Production

Highlights:

- Manufacturing should be need-based
- Manufacture of use and throw goods to be avoided/ minimised
- Cosmetic packaging should be minimised/avoided.
- Recycling/re-processing/re-manufacture of goods
- Include Human and Animal Energy under Renewable Energy.
- Maximum use of local material to reduce carbon footprint

As we humans have been consuming the natural resources and contaminating them at an alarming rate, the result would be that the health of the entire ecosystem would be lost leaving not only the present generation with issues but also future generations with inadequate resources and an uninhabitable planet. A glimpse of our production and consumption can be obtained by looking at the statistics over last 2 decades.

Current manufacturing and production system not only depletes the environment off its natural resources, but also results in enormous amount of waste that gets deposited in nature without being used, thereby polluting the environment and hence impacting the entire ecosystem. Thus, it is high time we re-look at our manufacturing and production system to make it sustainable not only economically but also environmentally and socially.

15.1 What is Sustainable Manufacturing?

Sustainable manufacturing includes:

a. Manufacturing of "sustainable" products, and

b. Sustainable manufacturing of all products.

The former includes: manufacturing of renewable energy, energy efficiency, green building, and other "green" & social equity-related products, and, the latter emphasizes: sustainable manufacturing of all products taking into account the full sustainability/total life-cycle issues related to the products manufactured

That means sustainable manufacturing is the production process in which sustainability is considered at all levels of the life cycle of a product in the 3 dimensions – economy, environment and society. Considering development and environment in silos will not enable the system to be sustainable. The major factor of a sustainable manufacturing is the elimination of waste that gets disposed polluting nature, and instead any by-product or product at every point in the product's life-cycle, enters into the nutrient stream as input for another process or product. A sustainable manufacturing thus help create a circular economy wherein waste is eliminated by circling back the products and resources back into the nutrient stream, thereby reducing the environmental and social impacts and at the same time providing economic benefits to the manufacturing industry by reusing the raw materials and reducing the quantity to be sourced. This means we design the entire system as cradle to cradle rather than cradle to grave – the former enabling the system to function as a positive closed system with no waste but reuse of materials; the latter wherein the system gives out waste and negative emissions, polluting the environment and resulting in loss of resources (as the waste released would get dumped in nature without being used) as well as requiring the extraction of more and more resources from nature.

15.2 Benefits of Sustainable Manufacturing

The benefits from having a sustainable manufacturing and production system is across all the three dimensions.

15.2.1 Economy or development dimension

- The effectiveness of the system and not just its efficiency is enhanced, as it caters to economy, environment and society in totality and not improve the efficiency if each dimension in silo
- Enables reduction in operational cost by enabling the reuse of the raw materials, energy and other resources in a circular fashion
- Increases brand value
- Regulatory constraints and thus cost is reduced or even avoided
- Avoids the operational cost attributed to waste management

15.2.2 Environment dimension

- The natural resources are conserved through the circular economy as well as protected from any pollution from waste dumping or toxic discharge
- Biodiversity of the ecosystem is retained with the availability of a healthy environment.

15.2.3 Society dimension

- The present generation needs are catered to as well as their health is unaffected from any pollution or toxic substances.
- The needs of future generation is also met as the natural resources are conserved and retained unpolluted

15.3 Methods and Tools for Achieving Sustainable Manufacturing

Such a sustainable system could be achieved by assessing the design, processes and operational policies through the entire life-cycle of the product – from raw material sourcing through processing and manufacturing through product transportation, consumption and disposal stages – towards eliminating waste of material, energy, water and avoiding negative emissions. Thus, Life Cycle Assessment (LCA) is the major tool or method of achieving the goal of sustainable manufacturing. The assessment should be not only across the manufacturing processes but also extend to the transportation and usage and disposal of the product by the consumers.

15.3.1 Material usage

The design should be assessed such that the materials selected for the product as well as for used in the manufacturing processes and product packaging should be bio-degradable or reusable or recyclable, that is, they should enter either the biological nutrient stream or the technical nutrient stream, the former allowing the material to be decomposable naturally, thus returning to the nature, and the latter being the reuse of the material in the industry either directly (say, by extraction of metals from the product for reuse) or by recycling (say, by recycling the plastic into a usable product). The design and processes should also be assessed so as to eliminate the negative emissions which pollute the environment or cause health issues for workers. Again, just ensuring recycling if not reuse of a material or the product is not sufficient to avoid environmental impact. But the design and processes of the recycling process should also be such that there is no resulting waste and negative emissions generated during this process as well as energy and water consumption should also be according to the below principles.

15.3.2 Energy usage

The design and processes through the life cycle, should be assessed so as to enable minimal energy usage through deployment of energy efficient systems for the processes as well as usage of renewable energy so as to avoid depletion of natural resources and negative emissions.

15.3.3 Water usage

The design and processes through the life cycle should also be that which enables minimal water usage as well as reuse of water through water treatment adoption. The use of non-toxic materials in the product design also avoids the contamination of water, which reduces the cost of water treatment considerably. The water treatment process should also be assessed so as not to generate waste and negative emissions nor any toxins.

Thus, a cradle to cradle approach for the entire life cycle of manufacturing and production is an eco-effective method and not just an eco-efficient method, as the latter is more superficial and short-term not really reaching deep enough (focusing on reduced usage and waste generation but not waste elimination), whereas the former is a long-term fool-proof method having its impact across systems and generations

Sustainable Manufacturing should involve some factors which should be given priority. It can be defined as follows: "Sustainable Manufacture is Manufacture that meets the needs of the present without compromising the ability of future generations to meet their own needs." Another definition is "For the purposes of Commerce's Sustainable Manufacturing Initiative, sustainable manufacturing is defined as the creation of manufactured products that use processes that minimize negative environmental impacts, conserve energy and natural resources, are safe for employees, communities, and consumers and are economically sound."

The present situation of Manufacturing is given below:

- Manufacturing industries account for a significant part of the world's consumption of resources and generation of waste.
- The Manufacturing Industry consumes bulk of the energy resources. It is estimated that 67% of the worldwide energy consumption is used up in manufacturing products.

Sustainable Manufacturing addresses the following criteria as at present

- Non-polluting
- Conserving of energy and natural resources
- Economically viable
- Safe and healthful for workers, communities, and consumers
- Socially and creatively rewarding for all working people

Manufacturing sector has the maximum potential for employment and remained so for the past couple of centuries and hence is a sector which cannot be ignored.

Nevertheless the Process of Sustainable Manufacture should evolve to higher levels. The Pollution from Manufacturing Industries has been regulated by various standards and regulations. However, the Pollution is still very high. Smoke CO2 and GHG levels are beyond sustainable levels.

15.4 Principles of Sustainable Manufacturing

Sustainable Manufacture should follow the following principles:

- Manufacture should be need-based.
- Manufacture of use and throw goods should be avoided/ minimised.
- Cosmetic packaging should be minimised/avoided.
- Recycling/re-processing/re-manufacture of goods should be given over use of virgin natural resources.

- Innovatively biomass based products should replace products consuming natural resources.
- Environment tax maybe levied for extracting and usage of natural resources.
- Increased use of human and animal energy in manufacture and reduction of Electricity and fossil fuel based energy. This will also give more employment.
- Maximum use of local material to reduce carbon footprint.

15.4.1 Need Based Manufacture:

Increased productivity awakens the hope of increased financial gains and increased income to the manufacturers and their allies. In order to achieve their end the products are wrapped in attractive incentives and Marketing techniques which lead to increased sale of the goods. On the other hand the increased production also draws additional natural resources. The depletion of these natural resources cannot be compensated by any activity and deprives the posterity of the resources. Need-based manufacture will limit the extraction of the natural resources.

15.4.2 Use-and throw Articles:

Use-and-throw items cause a surge of waste, which are dumped into the landfills. The manufacture is another source of dwindling natural resources. If the thrown away article are taken back by the manufacturer and reprocessed to renew the article then will cause carbon emission but the use of natural resources will be reduced.

Packaging: Most items are re- packed for convenience of despatch. Some goods are fragile and have to be packed carefully to ensure that the product withstands the rigours of transportation. Some items are packed for convenience of handling. Some items are packed only for better appearance than anything else. Such packing only reaches the waste basket on reaching the user, the worthiness of this packing is very less and unnecessarily some useful raw materials are used in producing goods of little value. Such wasteful products can be avoided to the maximum extent.

15.4.3 Recycling/Re-manufacture.

The Life Cycle of a product is assessed from cradle to coffin i.e from the initiation of the product to the final scrapping of the article into the waste bin. The cycle is natural for the items which decay or perish over a period. But for some durable goods this is not applicable. The rejected goods can be recycled to and new product can be made.

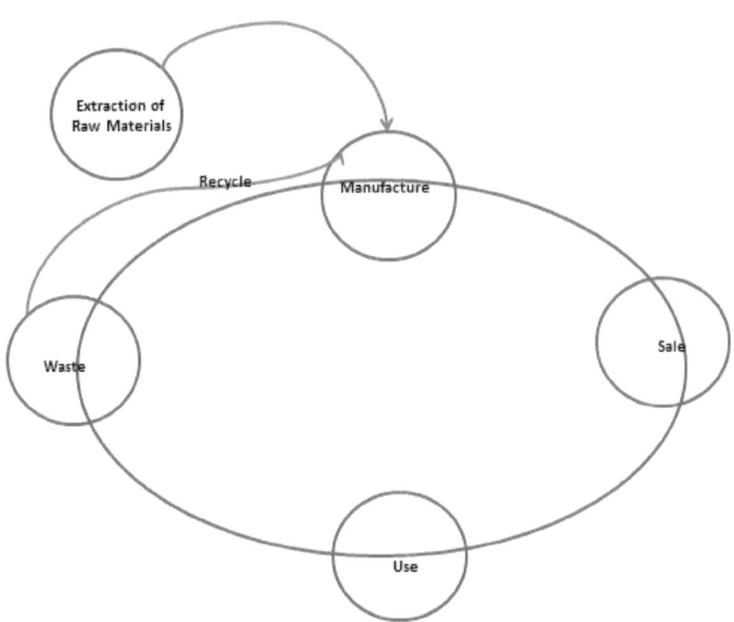

15.4.4 Replacement of consumables with bio mass based products:

Research should be promoted to replace the existing consumables with biomass based products which are renewable. For example biomass based cement has been formulated in the laboratories which can be further advanced to be made into a scalable product.

15.4.5 Environment Tax on Use of Natural Resources

Environment tax should be applicable on extraction of natural resource. This would be disincentive for use of natural resources. The taxes should be telescopic and increased usage of the natural resources may be subject to higher taxes to limit the extraction.

14.5.6 Human and Animal Energy as Renewable Sources

Human and animal power are the forgotten renewables which we need to re-focus on and treated as such.

Globally, there is still widespread dependence on traditional forms of energy, and human and animal power still contribute a significant proportion of the energy used in the rural areas of developing countries.

After biomass, they are the most important energy sources for their populations. On a global scale, the energy contributed by human and animal power is estimated to be twice that of wind power and 13% of hydro, the largest single contributor of the renewable energy sources. Therefore human and animal power should be included in the 'family' of renewable energy sources of solar, wind, hydro and biomass. There are numerous opportunities to improve the efficiency (and output) of hand, foot and animal-powered equipment.

Improvements in these technologies will help to reduce the drudgery and hardship of everyday life of those who do not have access to modern forms of energy. Such improvements will then lead to minimisation of fossil fuel based energy and also help in employment generation.

16

Sustainable Tourism

> ***Highlights:***
>
> - Establishment of "Sustainable Tourism Authority of India"
> - Integrating Education with Tourism
> - Implementing UN SD Goals at wards and village levels through tourism.

Sustainable tourism is defined by the UN Environment Program (UNEP) and UN World Tourism Organization (UNWTO) as "tourism that takes full account of its current and future economic, social and environmental impacts, addressing the needs of visitors, the industry, the environment and host communities."

Sustainable Tourism refers to sustainable practices in and by the tourism industry. It is an aspiration to acknowledge all impacts of tourism, both positive and negative. It aims to minimize the negative impacts and maximize the positive ones.

Negative impacts to a destination include economic leakage, damage to the natural environment and overcrowding to name a few.

Positive impacts to a destination include job creation, cultural heritage preservation and interpretation, wildlife preservation landscape restoration, and more.

Additionally, they say that sustainable tourism "refers to the environmental, economic, and socio-cultural aspects of tourism development, and a suitable balance must be established between these three dimensions to guarantee its long-term sustainability"

16.0 Sustainable Tourism – Indian Scenario

India rank poorly in sustainability although it has grown consistently to reach 13th rank in the world in terms of International Tourism Receipts and 22nd rank in terms of International Tourist Arrivals as per UNWTO data for the year 2019, but its rank under Environmental Sustainability has been 139, 134 and 128 in the year 2015,2017 and 2019 respectively. It shows India's poor track record in sustainable tourism. India is also not a preferred destination for nature tourism.

Ministry of Tourism has recognised the immense potential of sustainable tourism in becoming a source of sustainable livelihoods in a high population scenario, and has given a special focus on promoting 'Incredible India' brand to attract tourists, not only to major cities and heritage attractions, but also to rural India where through correctly aligned policy mechanisms, the problems of disguised unemployment in agriculture as well as migration to urban areas can be mitigated through community based tourism models.

Moreover, tourism is one of the few service sectors operating in rural areas and other fragile ecosystems, where the conservation of cultural heritage also becomes an important facet apart from the natural heritage. There is a need to create a sustainable balance between visitor numbers and heritage conservation towards sustainable use of resources and mitigating negative impacts on environment and society.

With the institutionalization of Global Sustainable Tourism Council (GSTC) in 2010, the Ministry of Tourism undertook to adopt the GSTC criteria for sustainable tourism in the Indian context.

16.1 Aims of Sustainable Tourism

UNEP and UNWTO in their joint publication in "Making Tourism More Sustainable: A guide for policy makers" have laid down the twelve aims for sustainable tourism:

i. Economic Viability

To ensure the viability and competitiveness of tourism destinations and enterprises, so that they are able to continue to prosper and deliver benefits in the long term.

ii. Local Prosperity

To maximize the contribution of tourism to the economic prosperity of the host destination, including the proportion of visitor spending that is retained locally.

iii. Employment Quality

To strengthen the number and quality of local jobs created and supported by tourism, including the level of pay, conditions of service and availability to all without discrimination by gender, race, disability or in other ways.

iv. Social Equity

To seek a widespread and fair distribution of economic and social benefits from tourism throughout the recipient community, including improving opportunities, income and services available to the poor.

v. Visitor Fulfilment

To provide a safe, satisfying and fulfilling experience for visitors, available to all without discrimination by gender, race, and disability or in other ways.

vi. Local Control

To engage and empower local communities in planning and decision making about the management and future development of tourism in their area, in consultation with other stakeholders.

vii. Community Wellbeing

To maintain and strengthen the quality of life in local communities, including social structures and access to resources, amenities and life support systems, avoiding any form of social degradation or exploitation.

viii. Cultural Richness

To respect and enhance the historic heritage, authentic culture, traditions and distinctiveness of host communities.

ix. Physical Integrity

To maintain and enhance the quality of landscapes, both urban and rural, and avoid the physical and visual degradation of the environment.

x. Biological Diversity

To support the conservation of natural areas, habitats and wildlife, and minimize damage to them.

xi. Resource Efficiency

To minimize the use of scarce and non-renewable resources in the development and operation of tourism facilities and services.

xii. Environmental Purity

To minimize the pollution of air, water and land and the generation of waste by tourism enterprises and visitors.

The order in which these twelve aims are listed does not imply any order of priority. Each one is equally important.

16.2 Terms related to Sustainable Tourism

16.2.1 Ecotourism

Ecotourism is a niche segment of tourism in natural areas. The term emerged in the late 1980s.

Fennell described it as such: "Ecotourism is a sustainable form of natural resource-based tourism that focuses primarily on experiencing and learning about nature, and which is ethically managed to be low-impact, non-consumptive, and locally-oriented. It typically occurs in natural areas, and should contribute to the conservation or preservation of such areas" (Fennell, 1999: 43. *Ecotourism: An Introduction*).

The Mohonk Agreement (2000), a proposal for international certification of Sustainable Tourism and Ecotourism, saw ecotourism as "sustainable tourism with a natural area focus, which benefits the environment and communities visited, and fosters environmental and cultural understanding, appreciation, and awareness."

The ecotourism definition by the Global Ecotourism Network (GEN): "Ecotourism is responsible travel to natural areas that conserves the environment, sustains the well-being of the local people, and creates knowledge and understanding through interpretation and education of all involved (visitors, staff and the visited)."

16.2.2 Responsible Travel

Responsible Travel refers to the behavior of individual travellers aspiring to make choices according to sustainable tourism practices. The behaviors usually align with minimizing the negative impacts and maximizing positive ones when one visits a tourism destination.

Travellers that want to learn more about how to be a responsible traveller can visit the section on the GSTC website for Travellers.

Summary of the difference between Sustainable Tourism, Ecotourism, and Responsible Travel

Ecotourism is a niche segment of tourism in natural areas.

Sustainable Tourism *does not* refer to a specific type of tourism, rather it is an aspiration for the impacts of all forms of tourism to be sustainable for generations to come.

Responsible Travel is a term referring to the behavior and style of individual travelers. The behaviors align with making a positive impact to the destination rather than negative ones.

16.3 Sustainable Tourism and the GSTC Criteria

The GSTC Criteria serve as the global standards for sustainability in travel and tourism. The Criteria are used for education and awareness-raising. They're used for policy-making, measurement and evaluation reasons and as a basis for certification.

They are the result of a worldwide effort to develop a common language about sustainability in tourism. They are categorized in four pillars:

A. Sustainable management;

B. Socioeconomic impacts;

C. Cultural impacts;

D. Environmental impacts.

These standards were built on decades of prior work from industry experts around the globe. During the process of development, they were widely consulted in both developed and developing countries. They reflect our goal in attaining a global consensus on sustainable tourism.

The process of developing the Criteria was designed to adhere to the standards-setting code of the ISEAL Alliance. The ISEAL Alliance is the international body providing guidance for the management of sustainability standards in all sectors. That code is informed by relevant ISO standards.

Finally, the GSTC Criteria are the starting goals that businesses, governments, and destinations should achieve. Tourism destinations each have their own culture, environment, customs, and laws. Therefore, the Criteria are designed to be adapted to local conditions and supplemented by additional criteria for the specific location and activity.

There are two sets of Criteria

1. GSTC Industry Criteria = relates to the sustainable management of private sector travel industry, focusing currently on Hotels and Tour Operators.
2. GSTC Destinaqtion Criteria = relates to sustainable management of Tourism Destinations.

16.4 Suggestions of Mission Sustainable India to Promote "Sustainable Tourism"

To implement the GSTC criteria, elaborate multiple institutional arrangement is needed to be in place which might itself be unsustainable for a country like India. Instead of multiple agencies, we suggest the following measures:

1. Establishment of "Sustainable Tourism Authority of India"
2. Integrating Education with Tourism
3. Implementing UN SD Goals at wards and village levels through tourism.

16.4.1 Establishment of "Sustainable Tourism Authority of India"

The Central Government may establish a single agency to be named as "Sustainable Tourism Authority of India", under the Ministry of Tourism and mandate it with preparation and implementation of Sustainable Tourism plans for local, regional and nation levels. The authority may also be entrusted with powers to issue guidelines to the respective local and state level agencies having a role in the tourism sector.

The Authority may work both for Industry as well as Destination.

16.4.2 Integrating Education with Tourism

As recommended under the Chapter-8 on "Sustainable Education", (Volume-2 of the Vision Document), the formal education system disconnects the children from nature, communities, local languages, wisdom and real world issues.

The class room learning cannot create the experience which the outside real life spaces can provide.

There is already a trend emerging where the families are coming together and forming 'Travel Communities'. They handhold each other and take steps outside the classroom into the world of travelling, experiential, integrated learning, exploration and connection.

They co-create connections, networks, and constellations for traveling and educating themselves through combined curiosity and connect as WORLD FAMILY-**वसुधैव कुटुम्बकम् शैक्ष्यम्** which means Learning with the World Family.

Facebook page link of one such group is given below for reference:

https://www.facebook.com/groups/learningbytraveling/permalink/4255886993876 80/

16.4.3 Implementing UN SD Goals at wards and village levels through tourism.

Localization of UN SD Goals such as 'No Poverty', 'Zero Hunger', 'Clean Water and Sanitation' 'Clean Energy' etc. at wards and village levels is possible if these are integrated with promotion of Eco-tourism, Village Tourism.

www.ingramcontent.com/pod-product-compliance
Ingram Content Group UK Ltd.
Pitfield, Milton Keynes, MK11 3LW, UK
UKHW042014190726
13854UKWH00005B/2279